Dopefiend's Redemption

Jim Gilbert

First Edition

Published in 2020 by
Bridge Builder Press
47 Cleveland Street
Orange, NJ 07050

Cover and book design:
Keith Kinsella, Tiger Paw Design

ISBN: 978-0-578-74789-7

BRIDGEBUILDER PRESS
publishing in New Jersey since 1976

This book is dedicated to the memory of my beloved son: Brian Jeffrey Gilbert.

A Publication of the Maggie INK Project

The publishing of this book, *Dopefiend's Redemption*, has been made possible by the support of the Maggie INK Project. This Project was established at the University of Orange by co-founder Maggie Thompson. Maggie published her own memoir, *From One to Ninety-One: A Life*, when she was 91. She said the writing of that book was, "...a rescue of my life. I crave this for other people who are poor or elderly. If you just start writing, you will feel better."

Jim Gilbert was chosen as the 2020 Maggie INK award winner. The Project raised the money to publish *Dopefiend's Redemption*.

CONTENTS

CONTENTS

PROLOGUE

Ilene wakes me at midnight, "Kalief is gone. He committed suicide this afternoon."

Shock and grief sit side by side in my mind. This could not be true. My attempt at disbelief fails. Is this pain physical or emotional? It doesn't matter. Kalief is dead. I hurt. Sleep is not possible.

I tearfully dwell on disturbing questions the remainder of the night. Why did Kalief have to die? Why did I survive and not Kalief? I had squandered the formative years of my adulthood in pursuit of self-gratification and addiction, as compared to Kalief, who endured and survived a terrifying, life-threatening experience with grace and dignity. Kalief was a good man—kind, respectful of others, and highly intelligent. He was destined for greatness had he lived.

Kalief's death was directly related to his having spent three years in Rikers Island for a crime that he did not commit. The resulting Post-Traumatic Stress Disorder and suicide attempt brought him to the Fordham-Tremont Community Mental Health Center, where I worked as a social work supervisor.

Kalief didn't talk much, but his quiet, pleasant demeanor and respect for others, coupled with a noteworthy intellectual curiosity, engendered an unmistakable fondness from all who knew him at Fordham-Tremont. Soft-spoken, but not timid, he had the ability to express himself with an economy of words in clear and succinct language. After completing the psychosocial, Kalief pointed out pictures of my two

African-American sons. "Is your wife black?" he asked. After I told him they were adopted, he smiled and said, "That's cool." He was a really nice kid.

As time went on, Kalief would often stop by my office after seeing his therapist. I believe that we both enjoyed these visits, an example of why I loved my work; I had no intention of retiring. However, as part of a "corrective action" in response to a client's (Kalief's) suicide, I got fired. I thought, "What am I going to do? I'm an old man who can't practice social work, my calling." I went home to Teaneck, silent, angry, and grief-stricken. A few days passed, and I had several serious conversations with Ilene and some of my friends. I came to the conclusion that in order to find purpose in the life that remained to me, and because of Kalief's death, I had to tell my story.

And so, I began recording mental snapshots from a long journey.

Part One
Troublesome Years

1. HELL'S KITCHEN AND RICHMOND HILL

My Mom was born in 1906, a child of Polish immigrants who settled in Hell's Kitchen on the west side of Manhattan. Her mom, my grandma, died before I was born. Mom told me that Grandma was always busy taking care of children and the home while being subjected to the unpredictable and abusive behavior of her husband. At the same time, she frequently sang Polish folk songs with a captivating soprano voice. But she had the misfortune of living in poverty with an active alcoholic who was often out of control with verbal abusiveness. Grandma's alcohol-infested home environment made it almost impossible for her to adjust to the cultural transition from the barefoot peasantry in Poland to the Irish-American neighborhood of Hell's Kitchen. She was afraid of this strange environment and consequently never learned much English.

Grandpa, on the other hand, became an honorary Irishman, spending a lot of time in neighborhood pubs where he became affectionately known as "Jake the Polack." Despite his alcohol abuse, he picked up English rather rapidly, both spoken and written, and became an ardent critic of capitalism, in general, and British imperialism in particular. Grandpa was a supporter of the Irish Republican Army and identified with the politics of Eugene Debs, a prominent socialist leader of that time.

My mom was the second oldest of four children. Her older brother, John, had conflicts with Grandpa, which, given Grandpa's drinking, appears justifiable. As the eldest male child from a dysfunctional family, he spent a lifetime attempting to establish order in his life and went on to embrace political and religious conservatism.

Uncle Stash, the baby of the family, experienced what was referred to at that time as juvenile delinquency during his early teens. While Grandma, Grandpa, Mom, and Aunt Helen responded with concern, Uncle John characteristically voiced disapproval. By his late teens, Uncle Stash rejected his anti-social lifestyle. Influenced by Grandpa's politics and in stark contrast to Uncle John, who affiliated with the John Birch Society later in life, Uncle Stash joined the Communist Party. He anticipated a life in service to the working class. According to Mom, Uncle Stash was well-read, remarkably intelligent, and maintained a working-class militancy without dogmatic absolutes until tragedy struck in his early twenties— schizophrenia. As the illness progressed, Uncle Stash could barely string two sentences together that had any relationship to each other, and his behavior became increasingly bizarre. This resulted in expulsion from the Communist Party, followed by a lengthy hospitalization and a complete loss of contact with the family.

Aunt Helen, Mom's younger sister, was a nice person. I remember her visits as a young child, but as my life became more dysfunctional, we lost contact. She married late in life, and like her two brothers, John and Stash, she had no children.

Mom did not have a happy childhood. In addition to poverty and Grandpa's alcoholism, tuberculosis struck her at an early age. This resulted in a back deformity and a need for a large back brace, which prompted cruel responses from other children. When she looked in a mirror, she observed a pretty blue-eyed blond-haired girl. Still, as the children's taunts increased, her feeling of deformity grew in intensity, impacting most of her childhood and adolescent social activities. Also, Grandpa was a nasty drunk who often verbally terrorized the family. Despite the chaos, Mom emerged as a person of kindness and wisdom. Starting in early childhood, she found a lifelong passion—reading. Mom once told me that when she finished a book, she felt as though she had lost a friend, and to compensate, quickly started another one.

4

In another world, Mom probably would have succeeded as a writer. A short story she'd written as a young woman is the only evidence that I have of her writing skill. It demonstrates an ability to create exquisite metaphors that resonate as poetic. Uncle John labeled her story "foolishness." While Uncle John wanted the trains to run on time, Mom wanted to help alleviate suffering. Although not active in a political sense, she was an example of personal, humanistic values. She listened to what people had to say and invariably treated them with respect.

Following high school, in keeping with the norms of the day, Mom acquired secretarial skills and went to work for the American Crayon and Crayola Company. Her boss, one of the few women in corporate leadership at that time, befriended her. (This was a time when the glass ceiling was a crawl space.) Following a visit to Mom's home in Hell's Kitchen, the boss lady advised Mom that there were better places to live. Mom agreed. She decided that she would save almost every penny of her salary, so she and her family would have a decent place to live.

Mom walked to and from work in midtown Manhattan to save subway fare—ten cents a day. Being short in stature and weighing less than one hundred pounds, she believed that she did not require much food and avoided lunch and coffee break expenses. At the same time, she avoided any excessive clothing or entertainment cash outlays. Mom endured, and, in 1929, went on to purchase a house in Richmond Hill, Queens—on a secretary's salary.

Shortly after buying the house, Mom met my Dad, a handsome, well-read man on the downside of a previously budding career in journalism and theater who showed her a world of sophistication and glamour. I entered the world in 1936. A year later, my sister arrived, and we all resided in the house that Mom bought in Richmond Hill—Mom, Dad, sister Ann,

Grandpa, Uncle John, Aunt Helen, and Uncle Stash. In looking back, it is clear to me that Mom and Dad's relationship, despite many difficulties, was a product of deep abiding love that lasted until Dad passed about 30 years later. In death, they rest together in adjacent graves in St. Charles Catholic Cemetery on Long Island.

The Richmond Hill house was a two-family, making it possible to rent the upstairs part of the house. For the first couple of years, this arrangement worked out well, the original tenants respected the property and could pay rent regularly. However, when they moved out, they were replaced by a troubled family whose out-of-control alcohol abuse and out-of-control children contributed to the virtual destruction of the house. It was 1938, almost 20 years after women gained the right to vote. Nevertheless, in 1938, women had little financial freedom, often needing a husband's permission to engage in financial activities. Therefore, Uncle John assumed the "manly responsibilities" of the household. He vetoed Mom's plan to rent to a childless couple in favor of renting to a family with children who he considered "more stable." The disastrous result led to losing the house and placing my sister and me in the care of other families.

Despite the good relationship she had with her boss at American Crayon and Crayola, Mom elected to obtain a civil service position for the state of New York, believing that it offered more job security than the private sector. Being a child of the Great Depression, she had little trust in corporations and looked forward to the possibility of belonging to a union. Mom went to work at Creedmoor State Hospital, where she could obtain employee housing; Dad moved to a furnished room in Manhattan while my sister and I went to foster homes. My sister went to live with a family of neighbors in Richmond Hill, and I went to live with a relative in a situation that is presently called kinship foster care.

2. BROOKLYN

It's 1939, and I have a vague memory of holding my mother's hand while walking along East 2nd Street to my new home. As we passed the corner grocery store, across the street from Tony's Fruit and Vegetable store, I had a sense of darkness. I guess that my Mom had explained to me that a new family was going to take care of me, and I dreaded the impending separation. The only additional recall from that moment in time was the presence of my cousins, three boys, and two girls. I remember that the boys were wearing white flannel pants. I also remember being restrained when my mother left without me, and I then began to develop the feeling that I was a disposable child.

I remained with this family for eleven years, never quite belonging. Throughout this time, I often fantasized about Mom and Dad getting back together and becoming a real family with my sister and me in a real home. Unfortunately, that didn't materialize until I was fifteen when it was too late and the damage was already done—more about the damage later.

Aunt Mary was a Polish immigrant who arrived in the United States at the age of fourteen, penniless and abandoned by her Ellis Island sponsors. After reflecting on it later in life, I think of how terrifying it must have been for a young girl in a strange country with limited family support. Like most Poles, Aunt Mary was a devout Catholic, which motivated her to seek guidance from the church. To this end, she secured employment as a cleaning lady and lodging in a convent. During her convent experience, which lasted until her late teens, she learned English and developed a love of reading that led to a lifetime interest in poetry. Despite its many contradictions, this memory reinforces my belief that service is a fundamental component of the Catholic Church, and providing a home for a young immigrant girl does not seem unusual there. At the age of nineteen, Aunt Mary transitioned from life in the convent to marriage with Uncle Joe, which subsequently produced five children.

Aunt Mary's formative years in peasant poverty and her later experience with the nuns resulted in a strong desire to help others. My memories of Aunt Mary include her frequent smiles and laughter, and her almost constant activity in one of her numerous undertakings—gardening, cooking, and making wine, cider, pickles, and fruit preserves.

Between the ages of four and six, when all her kids were in school, Aunt Mary and I had the house to ourselves. She always had a job for me, from helping paint the backyard fence to dusting furniture. I remember helping her fill a stocking with grapes that produced a batch of grape jelly. When not involved in a project, she read and, at times, would recite poetry to me.

Aunt Mary loved gardening. She expressed joy at the sight of new life in her World War II Victory Garden. I asked her why she didn't wear shoes when she worked in the garden. "I love the feeling of God's earth under my feet," was her reply. Years later, in reading South African scholar, Alan Paton's *Cry, The Beloved Country,* Aunt Mary's reply resonated: *"Stand unshod upon it, for the ground is holy, being even as it came from the Creator."*

For many years, Uncle Joe worked as a building engineer in the New York City garment district. He had a fifth-grade education, and his incredible engineering skills were self-taught. However, in all other areas, Uncle Joe professed an almost complete lack of intellectual curiosity. He rarely spoke. When he did, it was often to express anger and irrational opinions, particularly concerning race.

On a night in the early 1950s, the family was watching a boxing match on TV. A retired Joe Louis was introduced before the fight. After acknowledging the ovation, Louis shook hands with the two fighters, one was black, and the other was white. Uncle Joe became quite upset because Louis shook hands with the black boxer before he shook hands with the white boxer. Uncle Joe proceeded to display what later in life, I would characterize as irrational rage, with racial slurs. Even though I had little capacity for racial sensitivity at the time, I remember thinking, "This guy is fucked up." And my fear of him was reinforced.

Uncle Joe's character defects made it almost impossible for him to assume mutual partnership, and he relegated all decision-making in the administration of home and family to Aunt Mary. She decided that I needed a home and that she would provide one. While not directly challenging Aunt Mary, Uncle Joe made it clear that he did not want me in his home. He rarely spoke to me.

One winter day, when I was very young, I entered the house after playing in the snow and did not remove my hat. Uncle Joe did not address me directly. He looked at Mary, his youngest daughter, and proclaimed, "This is a Christian home. We do not wear hats inside." Pointing at me, he said, "He thinks that this is a synagogue." I remember with utmost clarity the shame and fear I felt as I removed my hat while making a supreme effort not to cry. I knew that Uncle Joe didn't like me and reasoned that there must be something wrong with me, which contributed to my chameleon-like manner of relating to others, especially to my "betters," in other words, people-pleasing.

Uncle Joe's mother (whom I called Grandma) was my Grandpa's sister, making the relation with my new adopted family somewhere around second or third cousins. In old age, Mom's widower dad (my Grandpa) lived with his sister, Uncle Joe's mother, a few blocks away from my new home on East 2nd Street. I remember him as a gentle old man who always had a present for me when he came to visit.

One time he brought a half-empty bottle of glue, some assorted colored paper, and some broken crayons in a cardboard box. I cherished those gifts. I have no recollection of his passing when I was about seven years old, but I do recall the joy and affection I experienced in spending time with him as a young child. Unfortunately, Mom did not have many pleasant memories of him, having directly experienced repeated manifestations of his alcoholism. He apparently experienced a "spontaneous recovery" in his mid-seventies.

Darkness arrived in 1942 when Aunt Mary took in an adult boarder, a young man who needed a home. Soon after he moved in, he started to abuse me. I firmly believe that having been sexually abused as a child is the basis for the self-loathing and character flaws that I experienced as an adult. Shock and fear led to embarrassment, a negative self-image, and a need to fictionalize who I was. I knew that I was disposable. I also knew that what was happening to me was shameful and not to be spoken about, a disgustingly evil activity that I took part in. When the pedophile arrived in 1942, my world started transitioning into increasing gloom and fear.

I believed that if Aunt Mary or crazy Uncle Joe found out about the sexual attacks, I would be in the deepest trouble of my life, sort of a variation of honor killings of rape victims among religious extremist groups. Self-loathing was reinforced by a nun who, because of my acting-out in school, often compared me unfavorably to my adopted family: "You should thank God that this family took you in, but you will never be worthy of them." Even Aunt Mary, at times, reminded me that my father was a bum. Although on some level, I believed that Aunt Mary would protect me, I also thought that she would never consider me blameless for the sexual activity I engaged in. I had to keep it a secret.

The pedophile and I shared a bed. He worked the late shift at Wolfe's Bookbinding Company in Manhattan and would return home sometime after midnight when I was asleep. He often awakened me to start the abuse. For a brief period, when I was about six or seven, I would attempt to sleep on the closet floor. I did this hoping that Aunt Mary would discover me, conclude that I did not want to share a bed, and move me to another bed without revealing the sexual abuse. However, the pedophile invariably discovered me, so my attempt failed.

Following puberty, I occasionally felt sexual pleasure in the abuse, which added to my determination to keep it a secret. I was about six when it started. It lasted until I left at fourteen. Asking for protection from this abuse was out of the question; in this very Catholic home, sex, whether consensual, coercive or forced, was a great evil not to be spoken about. I remember a friend who told me that he asked his mother where babies come from and received a slap in the face for an answer, symbolic of the cultural norm. Thus, the sexual abuse became a terrifying secret that I was sure I would take to my grave.

For many years, I labeled the pedophile a "faggot." However, I went on to learn that pedophilia has nothing to do with homosexuality. It is a mental illness that compels afflicted adults to seek sex with children. Right now, there is no treatment to eradicate pedophilia in individuals but there is treatment to help pedophiles control sexual urges; consequently, there are pedophiles who do not abuse children. However, despite the knowledge that the pedophile was a sick man, and despite attempting to pray for him later in life, I cannot find forgiveness in my heart. This man, whose thought processes were intact, had to know that what he was doing was evil. Therefore, I can only think of him as an unrepentant evil person. But with the help of healing communities, I was eventually able to let go of my rage. In addition, I believe that my desire to help people who suffer and my lifelong commitment to the profession of social work have their origins in the horror that I experienced as a child.

Outside of the darkness, I often experienced a brighter world and managed to retain many pleasant memories from Brooklyn. Stickball, football, stoopball, roller-skating, hand-ball, basketball, punch ball, box-ball, Ring-O-Liveio, and Johnny on the Pony were some of the activities that cemented an adult-free childhood culture—before the emergence of TV and the onslaught of technology. Although never quite com-fortable in my own skin, I had the thrilling experiences of childhood games and the companionship of many childhood friends, and these memories come back in *technicolor*. At home, with the pedophile and Uncle Joe looming in the back-ground, my world was in black and white and contributed to the belief that I was a stranger in a strange land. Indeed, the freedom that I experienced in my adult-free childhood culture was in stark contrast to the gloom at home.

Jane Bannon was a prominent figure in my brighter world. She was in my class at Immaculate Heart of Mary, starting in Sister Pasqualie's 1A in 1942, and culminating in Sister Jean Helen's 8B graduating class of 1950. I can't remember one single term where Jane's highest grades in the class, usu-ally between 97% and 99%, weren't announced from the pulpit during Sunday's mass. Despite these accolades, Jane's pleasant, unpretentious disposition stayed intact and she was well-liked and respected.

Jane was the only girl on our very competitive stickball team. She distinguished herself as a reliable batter and a classy fielder. Jane was a natural athlete who excelled in all sports, particularly stickball. She had an uncanny ability to place a Spaldine ball any place she wanted using a broom-handle stickball bat. Since she wasn't a power hitter, a rival team at-tempted a "Jane Shift" by bringing in the outfield to cover all infield ground. Jane responded by looping a fly ball beyond their reach, resulting in a home run.

Her sports career ended at high school graduation when

she joined the Sisters of St. Joseph, beginning a lifetime of service. As a nun, Jane went on to become a prominent educator, impacting the lives of many young women who otherwise would not have had an adequate education.

Mom's brother, Uncle John, often came to visit. He introduced me to places of interest—boat rides, amusement parks, airplane shows, and Ebbets Field, home of the Brooklyn Dodgers. In looking back, I shudder at the ungratefulness and disrespect that I bestowed on Uncle John as a teen. Eventually, we stopped speaking, even at Mom's funeral. For many years I thought that my dismissive and belligerent attitude toward Uncle John was justified because of his rigid Catholicism—immaturity on steroids! I now believe that Uncle John understood my Dad's limitations and the difficulty that I had with Uncle Joe. He wanted to be an understanding male role model. I now am truly sorry for the way I treated Uncle John; I owe him an amends. Making direct amends to a person who is no longer with us is not possible. Still, I can operationalize amends by trying to treat people decently, regardless of their politics or religious belief.

Uncle John gave me the opportunity to witness the Brooklyn Dodgers in their heyday. Jacky Robinson, Roy Campanella, and Don Newcomb were standouts who attracted many African-American fans. Ebbets Field was a 1940s anomaly. At that time, there was an unwritten law (de-facto segregation) that black people and white people did not mix. I fully anticipated that if black people went to Ebbets Field, they would sit by themselves. This was not the case. Blacks and whites were evenly dispersed all over the stadium, enthusiastically cheering for their Dodgers. Uncle John, a baseball enthusiast, despite his social conservatism, engaged in animated conversations with black fans. Unfortunately, his inclusiveness at Ebbets Field did not include neighborhoods, schools, or churches.

In fact, the only African-American that I had any contact with as a kid was Hampton Allen. Ham worked in Tony's fruit and vegetable store on the corner of East 2nd Street and Church Avenue, where I worked as a delivery boy. Ham was different from everyone else, and I felt different from everyone else too, so I looked to him as a refuge from a world in which I did not belong. In looking back, I can see that Ham, understanding the limitations of a black man living in a Jim Crow nation, intuitively understood my own feelings of not belonging. When I spoke of feeling different from my adoptive family, he advised that nothing is permanent, and the best is yet to come— words of comfort in my alienated world.

Before Tony's, I had a small business outside of the bank on Church Avenue and McDonald Avenue. I shined shoes. "Pete the Blaster" was a mob guy who owned the OK Diner across the street. I had the dubious honor of shining his shoes several times. I marveled at the fact that he was always impeccably dressed in a Zoot suit with pegged pants. The going price for a shoeshine was 15 cents. Pete paid his 15 cents and added a 25-cent tip. I was honored. I believed that Pete was an important man who was in charge of his world. He was a hero. Later in life, I realized that I always gravitated toward people who were apart from the mainstream, including criminals. Thankfully, I went on to recognize that Pete the Blaster was a self-centered psychopath, not someone to emulate, while Ham's overall message was that joy could be extracted from life. I felt accepted and safe with Ham, whom I experienced as a mentor. In contrast, I was awed by Pete.

Mom and Aunt Mary didn't like the idea that I was shining shoes, so I had to give up my business. Aunt Mary wasn't too pleased when I started to work at Tony's. Tony was a short, round, Italian-American with a perennial three-day growth of beard and a cigar clenched in his teeth. I'm sure that the reason for Aunt Mary's displeasure was related to ethnic

14

profiling. However, Aunt Mary witnessed Tony loading up a station wagon with donations of fruit and vegetables for the Little Sisters of the Poor. She heard the nuns thanking him profusely and witnessed him tipping his hat to them in return. After this, Aunt Mary thought Tony could do no wrong and that he was a good man, and she supported my employment at Tony's.

At the age of twelve, I discovered Charlie Parker on the radio, beginning a lifelong love of jazz. It turned out that Ham was a jazz enthusiast with firsthand knowledge of Charlie Parker, Fats Navarro, Dizzy Gillespie, Max Roach, Lenny Tristano, and many other bebop luminaries of the day. He introduced me to jazz radio—Dr. Jazz, Dr. Jive, Slim Gaylord, Monday Night at Birdland, and Jazzbo Collins. Jazz radio was exciting, often exhibiting "tongue in cheek" humor in addition to the music. Slim Gaylord and Jazzbo Collins continually provided smiles and laughter.

Collins deejayed a variety of jazz programs, including *The Purple Grotto* (traditional jazz), *Collins on a Cloud* (jazz ballads), and *Bring Back the Bands* (big bands from past generations). *The Purple Grotto* was home to a mythical 265-year-old owl named Harrison, who espoused wisdom but only communicated with Jazzbo Collins. Harrison would occasionally choose records to play; he particularly liked Bud Powell, Charlie Parker, and Miles Davis. One of my cousins wasn't too pleased with my interest in this music. "He's listening to that nigger music again," was reported to Aunt Mary, who dismissed the "accusation" as irrelevant.

At home, religious dogma prevailed. There was a miniature altar in the dining room where, in supplementing formal confession at church, one could humbly ask for forgiveness for sins committed, both venial and mortal. Venial sins were akin to misdemeanors and mortal sins to felonies. However, since everybody commits both of these kinds of sins, there is nobody on earth except "saints" that escape long-term punishment. In other words, we're all destined for significant consequences.

I never saw the pedophile pause before the altar. I knew that he sinned, but I also knew that his sin was my sin, so I had to keep it a secret. The resulting rage didn't appear until later in life when it grew to include the church and many authority figures, particularly during my mid and late adolescence. Thank God for alcohol and drugs! (Smile.)

I never heard curse words from any family member; even hell and damn were considered sinful language. Curse words were evil, while racial and ethnic slurs were considered a part of the accepted lexicon. Italians were referenced as *guineas*, Puerto Ricans as *spics*, Jews as *kikes*, and African-Americans as *niggers*. Although at the time I fully accepted this cultural proclivity, it provided a basis for future enlightenment. At a later age, this experience became a barometer to question hate speech.

Questioning racism evolved from a pronounced paradox. Aunt Mary, a serious Catholic, had a strong belief in service to the less fortunate. Although comfortable with the "N-word," she challenged racist norms. There were two or three homeless men who occasionally appeared on the block. At times, Aunt Mary provided them with food and allowed them to use the shower Uncle Joe had installed in the cellar. One of the men, Pete, was black. My friend, Jimmy Finnigan, took issue with this, remarking that Aunt Mary, a foreigner, allowed a "nigger" in her house. These remarks suspended all of my people-pleasing impulses; I was furious. I told Finnegan that I would rather live with a foreigner than a dumb Irish drunk like his father. We settled this dispute in a physical confrontation, both of us getting a few licks in before the fight was broken up by Mrs. Thatcher, a neighbor, who yelled, "You boys are supposed to be friends, and friends don't hit each other."

At about that time, around 1944, many inner-city communities began to change. Original white ethnic populations gave way to an influx of people of color. At the same time, neighborhoods became impoverished. Some Catholic churches closed while others adapted to the change by creating social outreach services. While our neighborhood remained all-white, neighboring communities such as East New York and Bed-Stuy changed.

Although Uncle Joe professed to be a good Catholic, he was a hard-core bigot, reverting to irrational rage whenever the subject of race came up. While caught up in cultural norms and not being adverse to ethnic or racial slurs, Aunt Mary was not comfortable with Uncle Joe's hatred. She was concerned about a trickle-down effect on her children, which is why she took me and her youngest child, Mary, to an African-American Catholic church to witness a newly ordained African-American priest celebrate his first mass.

Initially, I was apprehensive in the presence of all those "colored" people, incorporating lessons, both subtle and overt, that I had learned since early childhood. White was the norm, and black was the "other," invoking fear. However, I eventually warmed to the welcoming atmosphere where the spirit of fellowship prevailed.

The church sanctuary was present in other childhood situations. In the 1940s, church doors were open all the time, and I occasionally went into an almost-empty church, sat in a back pew, and contemplated a better life with a real home and family. There were usually a few elderly ladies in the church, engaging in quiet prayer, which contributed to a feeling of solace and protection—witnessing this priest's first mass produced similar thoughts. In addition to the occasional peaceful meditations, and despite skepticism, I've always loved church rituals, particularly celebrations during Easter and Christmas. I experienced this first mass at the African-American church with the same exaltation as I did during Easter and Christmas at Immaculate Heart of Mary. It was also similar to my first experiences in AA meetings later in life—I felt safe.

We arrived home from the church service and gathered in the dining room amid the faint aroma of candle wax, and we lit a candle in honor of the Infant of Prague that resided on our miniature altar. Aunt Mary, "little" Mary, Dorothy, two of the boys, and I were there. Aunt Mary reported our experience and was immediately admonished by one of the boys for bringing children to a "nigger" church. With the characteristic courage of her convictions, Aunt Mary silenced him with the suggestion that the next time he goes to confession, he include in his sins the fact that he referred to a house of God as a "nigger church." She went on to state, "I believe that is what you call blasphemy."

My first notable experience of religious skepticism occurred about the age of ten. It was a Friday, pre-Vatican II, when eating meat on Friday was a mortal sin, punishable by a never-ending sentence to hell. I did not believe that the punishment fit the crime. In direct defiance, I stole money from Aunt Mary's purse and proceeded to the Jewish delicatessen, where I planned to deliberately defy God's rule in the infidel's den. I said, "Gimme a frankfurter, mustard, and sauerkraut!" Thinking, "What are you going to do about it, God?" I clearly remember the young yarmulke-wearing clerk sternly reply, "Today's Friday, you can't eat meat. Here, take a knish." While eating my knish, I looked to the sky and had a word with God. "First, you get the nuns, priests, neighbors, and Aunt Mary to interfere with my life. Now you bring in the Jews." Despite this conflict grounded in fearful belief, I began to experience a healthy skepticism as to the existence of a supernatural being who created, controlled and determined all human events.

Like so many other young men of his generation, Ham

18

went off to fight fascism. He returned in uniform to visit the neighborhood and was welcomed enthusiastically as several older men took him to Patsy's Pizza joint, where they drank beer in an atmosphere of merriment. I remember feeling devastated at the lukewarm reception I received when attempting to rekindle our friendship. Although seeing Ham with his new friends reinforced my feelings of disappointment in all human relations, he remains a prominent teacher from my early life, a person who provided a semblance of sanctuary in a troubled world.

That night at Patsy's was the last time I saw Ham. I often think about what became of him. Did he, like so many young men returning from the war, benefit from the G.I. bill? Or was he subjected to the historical African-American reality of being denied access to government-sponsored initiatives that ultimately contributed to financial instability? The G.I. bill was the pivotal point in upward mobility for the white working class. Two of my male cousins utilized this opportunity to pursue an education that led to successful careers in commerce and law. Many other young men who returned followed similar pathways, joining the middle class. Before this, only a select few young men from the neighborhood attended college.

My own education began at Immaculate Heart of Mary grammar school, where the Sisters of St. Joseph provided basic instruction on the three Rs. Although it took many years to realize, the nuns provided a strong foundation for all of my subsequent learning, the very beginning of a love for the written word, and a respect for numbers. Unfortunately, because of the many contradictions between religious dogma and life's realities, in addition to the Catholic Church's pathetic inability to properly vet potential clergy members, I developed an increasing hatred for all things Catholic that lasted over thirty years.

This hatred of all things Catholic evolved from experiences with people like Sister Frances Stephany, a violent woman who enjoyed beating children, and Father Smith, an outspoken bigot whose breath often reeked of alcohol. Not to be outdone by Smith, Frances Stephany had a method for inflicting maximum pain while beating children. She would grab a shirt collar in her fist while pressing her thumb on the chin of the victim, exposing a greater area to slap while her cynical smile evoked terror among observers. As life went on, this habit of hatred and resentment spilled over into my relationships with less deserving recipients.

One day my Grandma was sitting on the front porch quietly crying. Aunt Mary told me to kiss her on the cheek and tell her that I loved her. I did just that and later found out why Grandma was crying. Henry and Harold Rosenfeld lived two doors away from us in our row house community. Harold was a standout player on our famed stickball team. Their grandma, Mrs. Rosenfeld, and my grandma were friends. Mrs. Rosenfeld, originally from Eastern Europe, spoke fluent Polish. Since both Grandma and Mrs. Rosenfeld were uncomfortable with English, their friendship blossomed. They'd huddle together on each other's front porches sharing Purim cakes and Easter bread over long conversations. This ended when Mrs. Rosenfeld died. Grandma wanted to go to the funeral and pray for her friend. Being an observant Catholic, she first checked it out with her church, assuming that under the circumstances, she would be given permission. Unfortunately, Grandma asked Father Smith. He responded that if she were to step one foot in that Synagogue, she would burn in hell. The tragic element of this story is that everyone accepted Smith's decision as valid and determinant. Smith was the same guy who denounced "mixed" marriages from the pulpit, referring to a marriage between an Italian-American man and an Irish-American woman.

Having almost no self-confidence or capacity for insight, I adopted a chameleon-like method of negotiating life by changing my persona to gain the acceptance of all people. Since this was impossible with people like Frances Stephany and Smith, I experienced them as all-powerful, so I erased all the positive elements of Catholicism from my thoughts, and this didn't change until many years later. Remembering folks such as Father Thomas Duffy and an Irish nun who taught the fifth grade contributed greatly to the gradual transition of my perception of the Catholic Church. I'm sure that if Grandma asked Father Tom about attending her friend's funeral, he would have encouraged it and possibly would have gone with her.

Father Tom was a veteran who had gone to war with his dog, a German Shepard called Frankie—Father Tom as a Chaplin and Frankie as a member of the K9 corps. They both returned to the community. I remember standing on our usual street corner with my "boys" and speaking with Father Tom as he stopped for conversation during his daily excursion with Frankie. We talked a lot about sports; Father Tom was a diehard Brooklyn Dodger fan. One memory that stands out is his humorous, self-deprecating reference to the cigarettes that we had hastily extinguished before his joining us. Within my alienated world, I felt accepted by Father Tom.

In those days, Catholic schools were organized in sixteen segments, each grade divided into two parts, A and B, each taught by different nuns. Frances Stephany taught the 4B, and the Irish nun taught the 5A. Significantly, I have retained graphic recall of Frances Stephany's violence while erasing the Irish nun from memory for many years. To this day, I can't recall her name, but following a long, drawn-out awakening, the spirit of her teachings returned. Her infectious love of poetry and her dedication to service came to mind.

The Black and Tans, formerly known as the Royal Ir

Constabulary Special Reserve, was established by the British government in the 1920s to repel Irish independence. Hastily assembled, it consisted mainly of unemployed, undisciplined, English working-class men who were more motivated by money and hatred of the Irish than service to their country— their principal goal was the destruction of the Irish Republican Army. The Irish nun's father, a farmer, was suspected of being an IRA advocate.

Related to this association, the Irish nun witnessed a contingent of Black & Tans descend upon her home, confiscate the farm animals, burn the house to the ground, and murder her father in the presence of her family. The Irish nun then spent several years consumed with hatred of the British. As time went on, she sought through prayer and guidance a means to let go of her hatred and establish an element of peace in her life. To that end, she prayed for her enemies, asking the God of her understanding to remove the hatred and discomfort from the hearts of the Black & Tans. In the process, she concluded that within the interrelated web of humankind, it is a sacred responsibility to speak out against injustice wherever it occurs, referring to the Ku Klux Klan as America's Black & Tans.

Despite frequent neighborhood tribalism, there was a strong element of working-class solidarity. Pete Hamill said it best: There were two absolutes in the neighborhood: 1) You vote Democrat and 2) You honor a picket line. Apparently, everything else was negotiable. The only time that I can recall Uncle Joe speaking directly to me was when, at about the age of eight, I crossed a picket line to get a haircut. Following the haircut, I returned home where two of my cousins and Uncle Joe were standing outside the house. One of the boys remarked that it looked like I got a nice haircut. I replied that some men carrying signs outside of the barbershop didn't like the idea that I was getting a haircut. The response was immediate and chastising, "You crossed a picket line?!" Knowing that I did something terribly wrong, I attempted to clean it up and replied that the men carrying signs were "guineas." Uncle Joe replied, "I don't care if they were 'niggers,' you don't cross a picket line." Even though Uncle Joe is one of my all-time least favorite human beings, I have kept his directive to this day. I have not crossed a picket line since.

South Brooklyn and surrounding areas, in the 1940s and 1950s, were gang-infested. Names such as the South Brooklyn Boys, the Tigers, the Gremlins, the Carrol Street Boys, the Red Hook Stompers, and the Bartels were an essential part of the surrounding geography. My immediate neighborhood was home to the Gremlins, of which I was a proud member, joining as a "Midget" and advancing to the status of "Junior" as I aged. In retrospect, I experienced the Gremlins as a surrogate family. Brooklyn gangs identified themselves as "Social Athletic Clubs" or SACs. In addition to occasional street skirmishes, we had a football team in two divisions that competed against other gangs (SACs) in the Parade Ground football league. My two seasons in Parade Ground football stand out as a cherished memory.

Some of my fellow gang members were without fear and on self-destruct while I was, at best, a follower. An incident from that time stands out. It was related to a serious conflict with the Bartels, a rival gang from "up the hill." The Bartels, armed with an assortment of weapons, marched down the hill on Prospect Avenue while we, the Gremlins, amassed outside of the playground, similarly armed, waiting for them. One of our leaders announced that we were going to "make mincemeat out of these motherfuckers." Fortunately, it was raining, so evidence of an emptied bladder was not noticeable on my jeans. I was scared. Just before contact, two squad cars from the 70th Precinct pulled up, and everyone dispersed. I was never so glad to see cops in my life. I remember thinking, "I'm glad World War II is over. I don't think that I could handle combat."

Gangs were different in the mid-20th century. Weapons of choice such as clubs, knives, fungo bats, and sharpened Garrison belt buckles provided an arsenal that appears benign by today's standards. The only firearms at a gang member's disposal in those days were "zip guns," homemade weapons, which were mainly ineffective and mostly unavailable.

In 1949, a young man constructed such an instrument in his shop class at Manual Training High School. Subsequently, a conflict arose between the South Brooklyn Boys and the Tigers, which culminated in a gang war in Prospect Park. The young man, being affiliated with one of the gangs, took part in this activity and brought his newly manufactured zip gun. During the battle, he fired the gun, mainly to instill fear in his enemies and display power. Unfortunately, the bullet killed another young man, which shocked the community and resulted in front-page coverage in several daily newspapers. A similar incident today would not merit much news coverage. Still, it typifies the underlying dynamics of low-income communities where crime, violence, and substance abuse often become part of everyday life, places where young men, feeling alienated, joined gangs for a sense of community.

Shortly after this incident, at the age of fourteen, I somehow found the strength to challenge my fear-based self-loathing. I refused to continue living in the foster home. Although I loved Aunt Mary, my shame and guilt increased exponentially because of the continued sexual assaults. I believed that I was involved in a disgustingly shameful activity, even if it was against my will. As culturally evil as sex was, men having sex with men was incalculably much worse, especially since, at times, I found pleasure in the abuse. I couldn't share any of this information with anyone and realized the only way I would experience any comfort in life was to leave home. It was time to go. In looking back, I realize that this decision was a major accomplishment. Unfortunately, for years, I'd continue to believe I was indelibly marked.

As I grew to adulthood, I repeatedly volunteered for situations that were not in my best interest, such as dropping out of high school and associating with morally challenged people. I sometimes think, "What the hell was I doing hanging out with these people?" But the thought emerges that I was no better than they were. As time went on, intimacy and mutuality vanished, replaced by a need to be taken care of; I did not have relationships—I took hostages.

After leaving my foster home in 1950, I moved in with my best friend, Joe O'Donnell. Joe was the third oldest of six children whose parents were Irish immigrants. The O'Donnell family presented a welcomed change from the foster home. My friendship with Joe O'Donnell began in Sister Pasqualie's 1A class and endured throughout childhood, where we experienced the journey of boyhood together, from a love of sports, adventure, and reading to first steady girlfriends and affiliation with the Gremlins. The friendship abruptly ended at the age of fifteen when I got arrested for car theft, remanded to juvenile detention, and subsequently kicked out of the O'Donnell home. Joe's dad thought that I was a bad influence on the family, and he threw me out of the house.

Years later, after reestablishing contact with our mutual friend, Joe Flaherty, I attempted, unsuccessfully, to meet with Joe O'Donnell as an adult. Flaherty informed me that Joe O'Donnell was now a New York City police officer; he did not want to meet with me. Flaherty explained that the Knapp commission was keeping a close watch on police wrongdoing, and Joe had reservations about hanging out with an ex-con. I suspect that he still had feelings about the disruption that I had caused in his home. Joe's dad often reminded him that I was a bad influence on his children. A few years later, after getting some stability in my life, I attempted contact again but was unsuccessful. I would love to see Joe O'Donnell again.

Joe Flaherty and his large Irish immigrant family lived downstairs from the O'Donnell's. An independent thinker, Flaherty challenged some of the backward and reactionary impulses of our white working-class community with what was later characterized as street-corner humor. With few exceptions, he was respected.

Mickey McQuade, a self-proclaimed authority on everything, was "lecturing" on the superiority of the white race while expounding on the nobility of the Irish compared to people of color. Flaherty interrupted, "The Irish ain't bad people. They're just as good as the coloreds, long as they behave themselves." A short time after this discussion, McQuade presented a rambling diatribe on white nationalism and American patriotism when Flaherty offered the opinion that the Soviet Union had a superior economic system to that of the United States. He praised Stalin for turning churches into museums and further contemplated that Immaculate Heart of Mary would make a great museum. This was Flaherty-style "street corner humor," which was later evident in his work as a writer. It resulted in a fight between Flaherty and McQuade. McQuade's face revealed the outcome—a badly swollen lip and a huge black eye that put a dent in his arrogance for the next couple of weeks. Joe Flaherty went on to become a successful journalist and author even though he never finished high school. I remember while Joe O'Donnell and I were still enamored with Mickey Spillane novels and comic books, Flaherty was devouring Steinbeck, Faulkner, and even James Joyce, who instilled in him a lifelong love for satirical metaphor.

Because of these working-class advances, Joe Flaherty's dad, an uneducated immigrant, was able to ascend to the position of foreman on the Brooklyn docks and support his large family in a stable community. At that time, two segments of ethnic employment divided the Brooklyn docks. The Irish worked primarily in grain transportation while Italians were predominant in unloading other cargo. There was significant animosity between the two groups. The Irish were labeled "Micks" or "Donkeys" and the Italians "Wops" or "Guineas.

Under the influence of alcohol at a Brooklyn bar, Joe Flaherty's dad proclaimed that he would never in life hire a "guinea" to work for him. Two days later, he was found dead in the Gowanus Canal. Following the requiem mass, in which Joe and one of his brothers served as altar boys, a muted talk took place among Joe and a few friends. One of the guys referred to the "guinea bastards" who caused Mr. Flaherty's death. Joe Flaherty responded that it wasn't the guineas who killed Pop; it was ignorance and hatred.

Following his dad, Flaherty quit high school and went to work on the Brooklyn docks, where he remained for several years. As time went on, "community control" of the New York City police department became a hot-button issue that was introduced by representatives of the African-American community in response to a long-standing problem with police brutality. Our neighborhood produced many police officers and firefighters, some of the two-generational variety. Consequently, the neighborhood sentiment was overwhelmingly opposed to community control.

Joe Flaherty, the consummate iconoclast, drawing on his intimate knowledge of racial insensitivity among white police officers, was strongly in favor of community control. Beginning with a letter to the editor of the *Village Voice*, this issue launched his career in journalism. A few days after writing the letter, Flaherty looked for it in a newsstand copy. He searched the Letters to the Editor and not finding it, became annoyed, and thought, "What is it with these people? That was a good letter, shoulda' been there." However, when he placed the newspaper back on the newsstand, he experienced the delightful realization that it had been printed—as a front-page feature article with a byline. A journalist was born! His success came to include political and sports columns in the *Village Voice* and the *New York Times* in addition to penning three books. Unfortunately, cancer, in addition to a life of heavy drinking, prompted an early death. The world lost an excellent working-class, Joyce-inspired writer who might have evolved into greatness.

3. ALCOHOL, THE ELIXIR OF THE GODS

Adolescence introduced me to serious alcohol consumption, starting a long-term romance. I remember my first drink at the age of six, a shot glass of beer. Most non-alcoholics don't remember their first drink, but a surprising number of alcoholics do. After ingesting that shot glass of beer, I recall feeling for the first time, comfort with life that hitherto I had not experienced. I knew that I would return to this beverage and eventually discovered that alcohol made me a good conversationalist, humorist, and better looking; it broadened my intellect and added a few inches to my height, a true elixir of the gods. Under its influence, I was no longer a square peg in a round hole. I belonged!

By the age of fifteen, I had become a blackout drinker. During a drinking excursion with Butch Callahan, a fellow gang member, we hotwired and "borrowed" a stranger's car, deciding to take a spin to New Jersey where Butch had relatives. I don't know how we made it across the George Washington Bridge since Butch couldn't drive properly even when sober. We managed to reach Hackensack, where we got arrested and remanded to the local juvenile detention center.

The juvenile bust marked the beginning of a long period of self-destructive behavior for me—bad decisions accompanied by an inability to learn from mistakes. Somebody recently told me that success is not the opposite of failure, but failure is often a prerequisite to success. In looking at my life from this perspective, I have been blessed with an inordinate amount of educational opportunities. (Smile.)

From the time that I first lived with Aunt Mary until I left the O'Donnell home, my Mom visited me every Saturday. I don't remember her ever *not* showing up. It wasn't until years later that I was able to recall the anticipation and joy that I experienced from Mom's visits. They invariably occurred on

Saturday when there was a lot of activity on the street. Still, as much as I liked the seasonal games, I faithfully waited for her to arrive outside of the Church Avenue subway entrance. And I walked with her to the same subway entrance when she returned to Queens. This is another example of an erased memory that reappeared during a reexamination of my life. Although Dad's alcohol problem conflicted with his ability to truly engage in a partnership and family responsibilities, Mom was consumed with guilt over placing my younger sister and me in foster homes. She consequently came to the rescue while I was confined in juvenile detention. Mom managed to get Dad to not drink for court appearances. She also secured residence in a dilapidated two-family home in a place called Polack Alley in Queens Village. And she presented to a judge that the Gilbert family, after years of separation, was reuniting in a respectable neighborhood where I would not be subjected to the antisocial influences of Brooklyn. The judge agreed, and I did not become a ward of the state.

Unfortunately, my sister had to complete the picture of the respectable family unit and was removed from a home where she was quite comfortable. She left Polack Alley three years later to enter a convent where she remained for the next fifteen years. In 1969, after leaving the convent, my sister told me that as a teenage girl, she believed that she became a nun to save her soul, but subsequently concluded that she entered the convent to save her ass. In those days, my Dad and I were not an easy pair to abide.

As my drinking escalated during my teen years, all other activities diminished. I stopped playing sports and couldn't manage to complete the 9th grade before dropping out altogether. While pursuing the status of employability, I managed to secure a job that overlooked heavy drinking. At sixteen, I went to work for the Jamaica Tent Company, helping to erect tents for county fairs, horse shows, and society lawn parties that involved traveling from the fashionable Eastern shore of Long Island to rural communities in Pennsylvania and other neighboring states. I loved that job; in retrospect, it symbolized a second major victory following the escape from the foster home.

When I began work at the tent company, I had neither the strength nor dexterity to keep up with my coworkers. Consequently, John Grim, the owner, decided to let me go. However, a guy named Sam, who was the foreman of the "colored" crew, intervened. He pointed out to Grim that the yard and the canvas room were in a constant state of disorder, making it challenging to procure material and equipment in a timely manner before embarking on assignments. He further indicated that although I was useless on a work crew, I was prone to do what I was told and would conceivably help provide a semblance of order out of the current disorder. Grim, being an astute businessman, understood that efficiency is positively correlated with profit. He subsequently reduced my pay from $1.25 per hour to $1.15 per hour and reinstated me with the new job title as "yard boy." In addition to various custodial duties, I was charged with the organization of the canvas room, which entailed keeping heavy tent sections in their proper bins.

Still smarting from the "demotion," I decided to make a supreme effort to be reinstated on a work crew. The ability to drive stakes into the ground with a twelve-pound sledgehammer is a crucial skill associated with tent work. My propensity to miss stakes and break sledgehammer handles was the main reason for my demotion. Therefore, I knew that to reach my goal, I had to substantially increase my ability with the sledgehammer. To that end, I drew an X on a tree stump in the yard and practiced hitting it with the sledgehammer. After a month of this practice, drawing on the experience of swinging a stickball bat, I got to a point where I could accurately hit the X continuously from a roundhouse swing, not only with both hands, but with either hand. In the process, I gained upper body strength and dexterity, which became noticeable. Before the end of the season, I was not only reinstated but advanced to the prestigious horse show crew. The accompanying self-confidence convinced me that I could work like a man and drink like a man, but deluded me into thinking that, in fact, I was a man. I was a child nowhere near ready for adult responsibility. I later discovered that it's hard to grow up as a child, but even harder to grow up as an adult.

Around the time of my 17th birthday, I got arrested for drunk and disorderly conduct. Unfortunately, I was still on probation for the juvie bust two years earlier, and my probation officer, Mr. Poole, began to use words like "incorrigible." He ultimately gave me a choice—either military service or jail. Although I chose military service, the decision was not well thought out. The new Air Force uniforms were a nice shade of blue as opposed to drab khaki, so I engaged the services of an Air Force recruiter and was inducted into the United States Air Force in February of 1953.

I did not do well in the military. Still, I managed to manipulate an honorable discharge based on "family dependency" in early 1955, two years before my tour of duty should have ended. My military career reinforced a budding interest in marijuana and introduced me to heroin. After discharge, I returned to my parents' home in Polacks Alley, went back to work in the tent company, and pursued my newfound interest in heroin. Although previously defining alcohol as the elixir of the gods, I was in complete agreement with an associate who proclaimed that if the good Lord ever made anything better than heroin, he must have kept it for himself. I finally had an identity—dopefiend. I'm certain that the excessive needle sharing during that period resulted in the appearance of Hepatitis C years later. I was fortunate to have recovered from this illness without a liver transplant, but it took several courses of very difficult treatment spanning three years, during a time when I was in stable recovery from substance dependence. Addiction has staying power.

One day, I was working in the yard at the tent company, and I found a roll of bills totaling $140. I thought, "This is indeed my lucky day!" I immediately made plans to purchase an ounce of heroin, which went for $100. (Minimum wage was 75 cents an hour.) At that moment, I noticed my old benefactor, Sam, with tears in his eyes. He'd lost a week's pay and was devastated. The roll of bills was his. I returned it to him. He picked me up in an embrace while planting a kiss on my cheek, exclaiming, "You my friend, as long as you white, an' I know you ain't never gonna turn black." That moment and those words have stayed with me all these years with utter clarity, often bringing a sense of joy and peace.

I remained at the tent company and continued to live with my family in Polack Alley until the work interfered with my addiction. This is an example of the axiomatic law of addiction: Non-addicts generally change behavior to meet responsibilities while addicts change responsibilities to meet behavior. Based on this reasoning, I concluded that drugs and alcohol were not my problem; it was the environment. I decided to move to California, where I would begin a new life.

I was 19 years old when I started my journey to Lexington, Kentucky, the home of the only government-sponsored drug treatment facility available in 1956. A nurse pointed out an old dopefiend, Coney Island Max. Max must have been in his 60s and shuffled around in his paper slippers with drool on his chin. "Is that what you want to look like when you get old?" the nurse asked. I wasn't able to comprehend that message as my perceptions were focused on the immediate. I couldn't imagine getting old. After completing the detox, I proceeded to Los Angeles, the first of a series of what is euphemistically deemed a "geographic cure."

4. ODYSSEY

In 1956, at the age of 20, I arrived in the land of palm trees and perennial spring full of hope, I later realized that this was the "magical thinking" variety of hope. As in subsequent travels, I brought with me the baggage of immaturity and an affinity for intoxicating substances. Nevertheless, Southern California seemed delightful at first. It was much cleaner than New York, and West Coast Jazz (in its heyday in 1956), promised an exciting experience.

I soon found lodging in a modest rooming house and discovered that two guys I had known in New York shared the same dwelling: Frank and Mickey. They were transplanted dopefiends, who were also on a geographic like me. What a coincidence! Frank, recently released from a New York state prison, hung up his parole in search of a better life 3,000 miles away from the authorities who'd locked him up. Mickey went along for the ride. Together, we discovered California wine, available at a dollar a gallon, and a weed connection. There we were, three transplanted dopefiends, substituting wine and pot for heroin. In the beginning, there were fun times, and we did not pursue heroin because I thought I was cured.

The good times didn't last too long. I discovered that Frank was not a very nice person, even by my standards. He was arrogant, demanding, and petty. One night, after he, Mikey, and I drank most of a gallon of wine, Frank announced that he was going to sleep and that Mickey and I were not to touch the remaining wine, as it belonged to him. "I'm going to sleep with one eye opened, and if either of you touches that wine, we're going to fight." Frank and I exchanged words until I finally relented. I said, "You can have the wine Frankie," as I crashed the wine bottle over his head. His bed became a receptacle for the spilled wine and the blood from a large gash on his forehead. Mickey drove Frank to the emergency room, where he got stitched up. I moved out the next day. I knew that Frank had good reason to avoid contact with the criminal justice system and would not pursue assault charges. I felt no remorse, but I was scared. Frank was a sneak who once boasted, "I don't get mad; I get even."

I soon found new lodging in another rooming house and ultimately concluded that something was missing from my life that could only be ameliorated by "a good shot a' dope." The main problem was that wine and pot were cheap and available while dope was expensive and hard to procure. The financial part of this problem was initially solved with the coin contents of a cigarette machine and juke-box acquired in a successful burglary. Next, I had to go to a black neighborhood where I assumed that heroin would be available. I was right. I found a connection and resumed my interest in heroin.

At that time, I started to entertain the question of why dope was not available in white neighborhoods to the extent that it was in black neighborhoods. I thought, "This is unfair." I recall visiting an African-American rowhouse community to purchase heroin. The young entrepreneur who I did business with appeared on the front steps of his dwelling wearing jeans, a T-shirt, and flip-flops. He seemed to be comfortable and at ease in his environment while reaching into his pocket for packets of heroin bound by a rubber band. I purchased several of these packets and thought to myself, "Why wasn't I born black, where I would have easy access to this wonderful substance; why do colored people have it so much easier to enjoy heroin?"

Nevertheless, I began to pursue addiction California-style, not fully realizing that unlike New York, where drug busts resulted in "skid bids" of 30 days to six months, California prescribed long prison sentences for similar offenses. Therefore, I was quite dismayed when a neighbor said that police visited my room during my absence. To this day, I don't know what they were after, but my proclivity for ignoring laws suggested that if found by the cops, I would go to jail, perhaps for a long time.

I had to get away immediately, and this situation provided an opportunity to see the country from the seat of a Greyhound bus to New York. I arrived without the cumbersome responsibility of luggage—the clothes on my back as my only possession. Chilled to the bone, I headed for a familiar cop spot and was welcomed with sarcastic remarks such as, "Looks like you really did good in California—ha-ha." Nevertheless, somebody turned me on to a "G shot" (small amount of dope), and I returned to my aging parents, who at this point were not very enthusiastic about greeting their 21-year-old son, who needed someone to take care of him.

Back in New York, I was terrified by the dramatic increase of street violence and police violence associated with my heroin use, so I transitioned back to alcohol. I got a bartender's job at a local dancehall-type pub called Community Garden and found it to be even more accepting of heavy drinking than the tent company was.

I viewed bartending as not exactly a job, but a legitimate way to drink and hang out, reminiscent of the colloquialism "too lazy to work and too scared to steal."

Despite the downward progression of substance dependence, I felt a sense of connectedness at the Community Garden as it provided young people a sanctuary from isolation and felt like a surrogate family. I actually looked forward to work.

Jim O'Brian, Jerry Shanley, and Mike Kempton were my closest associates from that time. I wonder what became of them and would love to re-connect with them. They drank a lot, but were not criminally-minded like my dopefiend companions. I don't think I recognized it at the time, but in looking back, I can see that they were decent young men.

They were all bright, but Shanley was exceptional. Although he liked his liquor, he finished high school and ultimately went on to college, something that was rare among my associates. He wrote poetry to his girlfriend and was an anti-racist, also a rarity, which I thought was cool. We were both avid readers and had many conversations on current reads. Steinbeck, Hemmingway, James Jones, Kerouac, and Baldwin were experienced in a spirit of discovery. Both of us identified *We Fished All Night* by Willard Motley as a favorite. The one author that we completely disagreed on was Ayn Rand. I thought Rand was a great storyteller while Jerry Shanley believed she was a one-dimensional writer who produced comic book characters. Despite my interest in reading, I had some maturing to do regarding my choice of writers. Jerry Shanley's appraisal of Ayn Rand was on the money.

Like the situation in California, I started to crave something more substantial than alcohol and again began to "dip & dab" in heroin. People from the Garden did not welcome this activity. Eventually, I got fired, and friends from the Garden avoided me. I felt a sense of loss and abandonment that I still recall with sadness. Drugs came to the rescue while adding to a spiritual decline. I wasn't comfortable in my own skin, and the lack of capacity for introspection and insight led me to the conclusion that my problem was drug-enriched places like New York and Los Angeles, so I decided I would go to Florida where heroin wasn't as popular.

Consequently, the geographic cures continued, but I was not able to recapture that feeling of belonging that I had in the Community Garden until years later in recovery.

Shortly after I arrived in Florida in 1958, I got a bartender's job at the Flamingo Way Inn, a hotspot in proximity to Hialeah Racetrack that was patronized by a variety of free-spirit types. Complementing this good fortune, I found a drugstore that prescribed drugs without prescriptions. The joys of amphetamines, barbiturates, and synthetic opiates that paired well with alcohol were all mine. The Flamingo Way Inn became a bright spot. I was high all the time—amphetamines and alcohol during business hours, opiates and barbiturates during leisure time, in combinations apropos to various settings. The combination of "uppers" and "downers" provided occasional stability.

One night, after drinking much liquor and slurring my words, I swallowed a handful of amphetamine pills and almost immediately appeared sober. A guy sitting at the bar remarked on the change. I assured him that he was imagining things. Unfortunately, I wasn't always able to manage intoxicated states. One evening, while under the influence, I got into a fistfight with a customer. During the ruckus, we knocked over a table and broke a few glasses before two bouncers restored order. While customers were alarmed, my boss was seriously considering whether I had the emotional stability to stay on the job. Fortunately, the customer that I fought wasn't wrapped too tight either, and in stretching the truth, I was able to convince the boss that I was just defending myself from an attack. Despite occasional drug- and alcohol-related problems, I managed to hold on to my job for a little over two years.

Shortly after starting work at the Flamenco Way Inn, I hung out with an eclectic substance-abusing crowd of racetrack enthusiasts, jazz musicians, and various types of denizens whose unwritten code of existence was "live fast, die young, and have a good-looking corpse."

The Flamenco Way Inn was open until 5 am. At closing time, after counting tips and money stolen from the cash registers, a bunch of us would head for the all-night spots. With the help of amphetamine, the party ended somewhere between 10 am and noon. Large doses of barbiturates and synthetic opiates provided a deep sleep until 7:30 pm when I would start the process over again with amphetamine and coffee.

At the time, I thought that I had arrived. Lack of self-awareness and grandiosity shielded me from the lack of purpose in my life. In retrospect, I realize that I was in the end stages of a path without hope or promise, changing into a fictitious person. Gone was the ability to establish meaningful connections. There were no more Joe O'Donnell's, Joe Flaherty's, or Jerry Shanley's in life; all were superficial.

A glaring example of this moral collapse was when my friend Lynn passed. Amid the rollicking nature of our lifestyles—drugs, alcohol, jazz, and sex—we enjoyed each other's company. This freewheeling activity ended when Lynn was diagnosed with cancer. She returned to her hometown in New Jersey to be with her mom and family when her life ended. When I got word of her death, the first thing that I thought was, "How do I play this? Do I attempt to cry?" I did not feel a sense of sadness or loss; my emotional state was blank. I now shudder to think that I was a man without a soul.

The Flamingo Way Inn had a house rhythm section of three retired New Yorkers with bona fides to some of the greatest names in jazz. Frankie Bell, the drummer, began his career in close association with Louis Belson of Duke Ellington fame. Sam Krupit, the piano player, played with Charlie Parker and some of the top luminaries of the bebop era. Ed Schwager, a guy who could turn his bass into a percussion instrument utilizing the front and backs of his fingers, was a protégé of Ed Stafranski of Stan Kenton and Woody Herman fame. Many musicians frequented the Flamingo Way Inn, bringing their horns.

The late '50s jazz scene in South Florida was remarkable. It was the tail end of the "West Coast" scene where musicians such as Stan Getz, Gerry Mulligan, Zoot Sims, Buddy Collette, and Chet Baker were household names. Initially, I was introduced to jazz when, with Ham's guidance, I discovered Charlie Parker at the age of 12, and immediately became a bebop enthusiast. I began to experience the "cool school" in 1952 with the appearance of the Gerry Mulligan quartet. Within a short time, this expanded into what became an almost total preoccupation with what was then called Progressive Jazz or West Coast Jazz. I really loved those sounds.

Many of the West Coast school musicians were white. I was delighted—a lot of guys who looked like me were playing this beautiful music. At the time, I didn't fully realize that jazz was always way ahead of its time in matters of race relations. Historically developed by black musicians, white musicians were welcomed from the onset. Owen McNally, a prominent journalist and jazz historian, succinctly captures this phenomenon: "Through more than the first half of the 20th century, jazz provided a rare, virtually underground passageway through which many young white musicians passed on their way to discovering the richness and shared common humanity of black culture." (While in 1939, the Daughters of the American Revolution refused to allow the world-renowned African-American contralto, Marian Anderson, to perform in their facility.) Despite changes since 1939, in 1959, Florida Jim Crow laws mandated separation. Although I accepted some racist stereotypes at that time, I don't believe that I was a hardcore racist. Yet I accepted Jim-Crow Florida with an attitude of indifference. I was a white guy of the '50s, a racist who did not know he was a racist.

The late 1950s also introduced "hard bop," which, unfortunately, Florida hadn't caught up with yet. As opposed to linear tones and an emphasis on counterpoint composition as practiced by much of the West Coast school, hard bop employed broad tones and a move toward thematic improvisation, which I believe brought the music closer to its African-American roots. This was the very exciting transition of music introduced by John Coltrane, Sonny Rollins, Hank Mobley, and others far too numerous to name. To this day,

I consider listening to jazz, particularly the hard bop variety, one of the ultimate joys of life.

I might add that jazz is the only world-recognized American classical art form that did not come to America as a European import. I believe that its proper name should be African-American classical music. The background music in Florida stands out as joyful and life-sustaining. At the same time, abundant drugs and casual sex created an illusion of paradise where critical thought and curiosity about the world, in general, became unnecessary. It was a fictitious world.

I met Betty Ann McEvoy in 1960. She arrived at the Flamingo Way Inn in the company of three friends while on vacation from her factory job in Massachusetts. Betty Ann was born and raised in South Boston, a working-class Irish-American enclave. She was bright, unpretentious, and had a wonderful sense of humor. I immediately realized that she was special, not at all like the people I hung out with. Betty Ann drank with moderation and never even smoked weed. I realized that I had to be on my best behavior with her.

Although not a jazz enthusiast, Betty Ann loved music and was impressed by my musician friends who performed at the Flamingo Way Inn. We visited the Dade County Musicians Union rehearsal hall, where we listened to the prestigious Modern Jazz orchestra; it was an exciting experience for both of us. Betty Ann and I were almost inseparable throughout her vacation. We fell in love. At least that's what I thought it was—again, love vs. need. Here was the woman who would save me and give my life meaning. But I was a grown-up who was not emotionally grown up—incapable of true partnership. I don't think that Betty Ann realized just how crazy I was.

Betty Ann returned to Boston with a promise that we would reunite soon. One month later, she informed me that she was with child. In those days, out-of-wedlock childbirth was unthinkable, especially in an Irish-Catholic working-class family, so Betty Ann had no choice but to return to Florida, where we soon married and set up household.

Before our Justice-of-the-Peace wedding, I pondered the contradiction of my lifestyle and the responsibilities of being a parent and husband. I desperately wanted to be a normal person with a wife, children, and a real job. But I had zero insight into how I fictionalized most human relationships as a way of avoiding shame and guilt like when my friend, Lynn, died. However, I loved and needed Betty Ann, and to achieve my goal of normality, I decided on the day before our wedding to "clean house." To that end, I packed a box with the many pills in my possession (uppers, downers, and opiates) and delivered them to a friend's lodging in a nearby trailer park.

In retrospect, I realize that this really wasn't a "housecleaning." A housecleaning is when you flush drugs down the toilet. In delivering the drugs to a friend, I was originating an escape clause, which I promptly utilized. The next morning, anticipating my morning libation, I realized the dreadful mistake that I'd made and rushed to the trailer park to retrieve my drugs. My friend, a Texas hillbilly, was quite disappointed, but not only understood my impulsive decision, but also anticipated my return. It wasn't until years later that I understood the implication of this experience, a painfully naïve attempt to get rid of a complex disorder. I was to learn addiction is more powerful that a desire to stop.

My daughter, Margaret Ann, was born on April 8, 1961, when I was 25. She was a beautiful baby, whom I loved dearly. As the weeks wore on, though, it became increasingly apparent that maintaining family life and working at the Flamingo Way Inn were incompatible. Indeed, Betty Ann felt isolated and missed her extended network of family and friends in Boston. So, we packed up and moved to her parents' home in the South Boston projects, where she grew up.

Through the efforts of my friend Paddy Flynn, a former Boston middleweight, who at that time was retired from the ring and tending bar in Miami, I secured an introduction to Bat Sweeny, a member of the executive committee of the bartenders union in Boston. Bat provided a union card and a job at the prestigious Parker House in downtown Boston. Tending bar in the Parker House was a mark of status in "Southie," so my arrival in Boston was met with a degree of welcoming goodwill.

Since there were no drugstores above the Mason-Dixon Line that provided controlled substances that you could get without a prescription, I had to find a new connection. Furthermore, I had to maintain absolute secrecy of my addiction from Betty Ann's family; looking for drugs in Boston was out of the question. To solve this dilemma, I made frequent trips to New York via Boston/New York shuttle flights and was eventually able to get mail deliveries. (This was before the Internet provided this service.)

Betty Ann's mom, Peg, was a difficult person. When Margaret Ann was baptized, I said, to accuse a child of a crime committed before her birth is an affront to reason and justice. Peg exploded. Condescendingly, she referred to the lack of morality and intelligence that leads to such ideas, invoking her "faith" several times. Peg was barely literate, and despite her "faith," did not attend church, which led me to the conclusion that I was right, and she was wrong. It did not occur to me until years later, just how inappropriate I was. I was looking for a fight and a moral victory but got shouted down by Peg, a better fighter than me.

I did, however, get along with Betty Ann's dad (until the disaster). Red McEvoy was a wench operator on South Boston's docks. One Sunday afternoon, Red was on the phone with a friend. He said, "I'm here with my son-in-law," followed by a brief silence. He then said, while winking at me, "Well, he's a Yankee fan and a Polack, but aside from that, he's ok." Red McEvoy epitomized working-class humor and had an indefatigable zest for life; I really enjoyed our conversations.

I had a routine before my trips to New York to purchase heroin. I'd remove a set of works (needle, eyedropper, and cooker) that were wrapped in a handkerchief from my jacket pocket and would stash it under the baby's mattress. On this particular day, the cooker got separated and remained in my pocket. When I arrived at the cop spot in New York, I ran into a very large detective who proceeded to toss (search) me. I was quite surprised when he came up with the cooker, thinking that I left it in Boston, and even more surprised when he cuffed me. I said, "Come on, detective, give me a break; I'm not a low-life, I tend bar at the Parker House in Boston." He replied, "I don't give a fuck if you're an altar boy at St. Patrick's Cathedral. You're going to be one less junkie on the street."

In reverting to anger and self-pity, I actually blamed this mess on police misconduct. All they found was a cooker with "a satch" cotton (a bottle cap used to prepare/cook heroin with a piece of cotton ostensibly saturated with heroin traces). I reasoned that this was not enough to warrant an arrest. Nevertheless, I was arrested, and Mom came to the rescue with legal help that resulted in a two-month stay at a new drug program on Wards Island instead of a trip to Rikers Island.

Mom did not smile anymore, and the laughter that I remembered from early memories was gone. I was too self-centered to comprehend what my behavior was doing to her. She was disappointed and saddened. And I didn't have a clue. Betty Ann and her family were shocked and angry; I became history in their eyes. In looking back, I remember feeling abandoned. I was incapable of maintaining an adult relationship, always replacing mutuality, partnership, and love with need.

The program at Wards Island provided a respite from the

wreckage of my life. It consisted of 50 clients, two of whom were white. I relished the contrast from Jim-Crow Florida and provincial South Boston. At that time (pre-hip-hop and pre-R&B resurgence), jazz was considered mainstream popular music in the African-American community. My interest in jazz significantly contributed to genuine compatibility and comfort in that environment. In the process, I rekindled an interest in chess and learned the game of bridge.

Although there was one guy who was anti-white and had no compunction about expressing his sentiments, he was the exception. Thus, my experience at Wards Island raised the question of whether black people are more accepting of white people than white people are of black people. In my experience, many white people find the topic of race embarrassing, and completely avoid it or dismiss its historical ugliness by blaming the victims of race discrimination as responsible for their own plight. Although my stay at Wards Island did not produce any insight into my addiction, it did provide an education.

After leaving Wards Island, I decided to return to Hialeah, Florida, with the hope of reproducing my experiences at the Flamingo Way Inn—bad decision. Having a reputation for being consistently under the influence of mood-altering substances while exhibiting no evidence of change, my drugstore connection evaporated, and chances of gainful employment as a bartender were virtually nonexistent. I reverted to an alternate occupation that I was familiar with—petty crime.

This trip to Florida was different. The downward progression of substance dependence deepened. Although I missed the Flamingo Way Inn, I no longer felt a need for community—all psychic energy was locked inward. My closest connection to others was a partnership with another dopefiend, Tony, a transplanted New Yorker whose complete disregard for the rights of others was evident in much of his behavior. Tony related a story that demonstrated his sociopathy. While rifling through the drawers in a bedroom during a house burglary, a miniature poodle entered the room and began barking. Tony related that he smiled and said to himself, "What a cute little dog, I think I'll just take you with me."

Along with his pillowcase swag bag, he tucked the dog under his arm and left. He subsequently sold the dog. I thought that this was over the top. It's okay to steal property but not someone's dog. Nevertheless, I did not challenge Tony and continued to hang out with him.

During this time, I discovered paregoric, an over-the-counter preparation used principally to alleviate teething pain. Among other ingredients, it contains opium and camphor. While opium produces euphoria, camphor is an unpleasant substance if ingested and must be removed from paregoric to enjoy the opium in its purest form. To achieve this, paregoric is boiled to eliminate the alcohol and separate the camphor from the opium. Then it's siphoned through cotton, which produces an injectable form of opium. Unfortunately, it's impossible to remove all the camphor. Continued use causes vein blockage which has resulted in serious difficulties during medical procedures when my blood has been needed to be drawn—another example of the staying power of addiction.

Despite the interest in paregoric, I used drugs eclectically, never avoiding an opportunity to partake in whatever was available. This made me a "garbage head" and led to experimentation with a potent hypnotic. While under its influence, I managed to procure a doctor's prescription pad. The effects of this drug assured me that I was invincible. Indeed, it was referred to as "gangster biscuits" —allowing one to "leap tall buildings at a single bound." So, I had no qualms when I forged a Dilaudid prescription and attempted to fill it. Dilaudid is a very powerful opiate. I did not succeed and got arrested.

The reason for the arrest should have told me something about the quality of my decision-making. The fact that the prescription was bogus was transparently clear to the pharmacist—I misspelled Dilaudid. Having been introduced to the English language in working-class Brooklyn, I never paid much attention to proper word endings. For example, I never pronounced the "G" in words ending with "-ing." Potato and tomato were "potata" and "tomata." Therefore, Dilaudid became "Dilauda," and I spelled it phonetically, which resulted in my first trip to the Dade County Jail.

As in the past, Mom came to the rescue. I made bail and got a lawyer. However, my freedom didn't last long. Within two weeks, I was arrested again for a drugstore burglary and returned to Dade County Jail, this time with a much more serious charge. Zero self-awareness and lots of immaturity are roadblocks to self-examination. Although it was painfully apparent to Mom, I had no idea of what I was becoming. I believed that circumstances in my life caused my problems, but the truth was that self-pity, isolation, and a lack of empathetic regard for others were responsible. The man who had returned that $140 to Sam did not exist anymore.

Bail was not an option, and I remained in Dade County Jail for a year, fighting the case. While in the county lockup, I got word that Tony was found dead with a bullet through his head. I believe that his violent death was, in fact, an extermination.

At that time in the New York City boroughs, drug arrests were outnumbering available jail space, creating an acceptable climate for progressive legislation. Thus, Article 9 came into being. This piece of legislation stipulated that treatment be considered before incarceration for addicts in the criminal justice system. Since state mental hospitals were beginning to empty out, space was available. Although the law pertained to New York offenders only, my Florida attorney, after much negotiation, managed to shoehorn me into it. I got lucky; there were no draconian drug laws at that time, but more significantly, I had white privilege. If I were black, nothing on earth could have kept me out of Rayford Penitentiary. Incidentally, Article 9 of the 1960s does not exist in the 21st century.

Sometime in late 1962, I shipped from Dade County Jail in Miami, Florida to Pilgrim State Hospital in Long Island, New York. The ward at Pilgrim State was reflective of the jailhouse mentality in New York. A "tip" in jailhouse communities was based on group designations. There was a "white tip," a "colored tip," and a "Spanish tip." Interactions between groups were quite limited. While there were common areas, meals, personal space, and even therapy groups were segregated.

Since civil rights legislation, segregation is no longer generally perceived as separate but equal, but separatism continues to thrive in jailhouse communities. The unwritten rule among most prison authorities is that animosity between the races be maintained to preserve order. If blacks and whites decided to join forces in the pursuit of mutual interests, the powers that be would have a big problem.

"Burning," in jailhouse language, is a term that has its origins in the act of a white person puffing on a cigarette after a person of color puffed on it. The term was euphemistically broadened to describe any association with people of color. On TV, Frank Sinatra kissed a black female entertainer on the cheek and was roundly vilified by several white inmates: "Frank burns." Ironically, I believed that black and brown inmates were a better class of people than most white inmates, but I had to keep this belief a secret. The thought that racism explained the disproportionate numbers of black inmates began to incubate.

Obviously, all crime committed by black and brown people is not the result of inequality, and society must protect itself from serial predators and criminals, whatever their race. But, when 80 percent of New York state prison inmates come from eight New York City neighborhoods that have been victimized by planned shrinkage, crime and punishment need rethinking. Currently, the criminal justice system in the United States continues to reinforce racial antagonism. Article 9 doesn't exist anymore, and the United States, with five percent of the world's population and 23 percent of its prison population (that includes a disproportionate number of citizens of color), is the most punitive country on earth. National surveys reveal that five times as many white people use illicit drugs than black people, yet ten times as many black people are in jail for illicit drugs.

With few exceptions, the white tips that I encountered took pride in anti-intellectualism. Intellectual curiosity was more common among black inmates. Despite racial restrictions at Pilgrim State, I had the opportunity to form a friendship with a black guy named Kenny. I now know that I learned much from Kenny about how an intelligent, decent young man can acquire the mantle of a dopefiend, career criminal, and unemployable welfare recipient. This intelligent 29-year-old man spent eight years in jails and penitentiaries and did not complete high school. I often think of what may have happened to him.

My institutional experiences, such as in Pilgrim State, led me to think that racism often becomes a pathway to addiction. Years later, armed with this raw personal anecdotal data, I embarked on extensive research for a doctoral dissertation that examined racism as a causal factor among African-American addicts. I discovered that among a representative sample of white and black addicts, whites had significantly higher levels of character pathology than blacks, and blacks had significantly higher levels of alienation when compared to whites. Alienation is related to social pathology; character pathology is related to individual abnormalities.

Leaving Pilgrim State sometime in 1962, I decided that I needed another geographic cure. I arrived in Chicago more apprehensive than hopeful, but soon found a bartender's job and a dope connection. The job and my personal freedom lasted about a year.

In 1963, I got arrested for robbery, spent some time in Cook County Jail, and ultimately received a two-year sentence on the "Peanut Farm" in southern Illinois. While incarcerated, I avoided farm work by claiming that I was a baker, which got me a job in the bakeshop where I learned rudimentary baking skills. I also had occasional access to yeast, the principal ingredient in raisin jack, a strong alcoholic beverage that we called "buck."

Buck became the libation that periodically eased the despair of prison life. To avoid detection, I made a supreme effort to prevent blackout drinking. If caught drinking buck, my bakery position, and limited freedoms would end, to be replaced by farm work or work in the rock quarry. So, with that in mind, I made the herculean effort to limit the effects of alcohol to "buzz" rather than oblivion, which reinforced the erroneous idea that I could control my drinking any time I wanted to.

Despite personal precautions, I narrowly escaped severe consequences related to drinking buck. Mr. J., a correction officer in the prison bakery, unlocked the steel box that contained yeast, and measured and added the appropriate amount of yeast to a large container of water for the daily bread baking. As soon as Mr. J. turned his back, George, a hillbilly dopefiend with the reflexes of a tomcat, dipped his hand into the water and emerged with a fistful of yeast, used to make a batch of buck. In keeping with precaution, this activity was planned on a sporadic basis because smaller amounts of yeast result in smaller loaves of bread, which could arouse suspicion. So, caution was necessary for the making and in the partaking of buck.

At the end of a typical workday, the bakeshop crew assembled at the front of the mess hall and waited for the corrections officer who escorted them back to the dorm. The bakeshop workers resided in a dorm as opposed to a cell block. One day while waiting to return to the dorm, the bakeshop crew attempted to avoid the detection of Pedro, a Chicago dopefiend. He violated the rule of moderation in consuming buck. He threw up, and when the crew tried to clean it up quickly to avoid detection, Pedro became belligerent, loudly proclaiming, "I can clean up my own puke." This alerted a corrections officer, and ultimately Pedro got transferred to Menard State Prison, where he completed the remainder of his sentence in the rock quarry. It's a good thing that the breathalyzer had not yet been introduced. If it had been, the entire crew would have been in trouble.

However, in thinking about it, it wouldn't have been in the institution's best interests if we all got job transfers. We put out a good product—bread, cake, pie, sweet rolls, even Christmas cookies. Training other inmates to replace us would have created a big problem. We did, however, suffer consequences around Pedro's misfortune.

The "goon squad" searched the bakery to find a stash of buck. They took everything out of the cabinets and drawers and dumped it on the floor. They did not find our stash, but we had to clean up the mess. While indiscriminately tossing all baking supplies on the floor, they overlooked a stack of old bread pans behind the proof box. If they had searched them, they would have discovered that although the top few tiers and bottom few tiers were "sure-nuf" bread pans, the middle of the stack contained pans with the bottoms cut out, creating a vertical space to cure and store Buck. Converting the bread pan stack to a storage space was a difficult job, given the lack of appropriate tools, but it did save the bake-shop crew added unpleasantness. Following the cleanup, we all relaxed with a cup of buck.

Early in 1965, I received a letter from Mom telling me that my dad had died. I was playing cards when the letter arrived. I read the letter, picked up my hand, and resumed the game without the slightest reaction, believing that Dad was too insignificant to give it much thought. I couldn't realize it at the time just how broken I was; I couldn't experience life beyond personal needs. Many clinicians would consider this behavior indicative of borderline personality disorder. I relied on ignorance and lack of insight and mentally reconstructed Dad's image to protect myself. He got drunk fairly often but was never a "nasty drunk." But I thought that if he had done his job at being a father, I wouldn't have become a drunk, a dopefiend, and a loser. I didn't have a clue where the self-pity ended, and the self-loathing began. At times I hated my dad.

Years later, in a therapy session that took place in the early 1970s, I recalled an incident from 1955 that demonstrated Dad's sense of fairness and his respect for all people, prompting a reexamination of my previously flawed perceptions of him. I eventually concluded that, in addition to his flaws, my dad, Earl Jay Gilbert, was a man of wisdom and compassion. Utilizing AA's Ninth Step, "...made direct amends to such people who we had harmed..." I went on to recapture memories of Dad at his gravesite, said, "I'm sorry, Dad, I love you." In AA this commonly referred to as a prayerful Ninth Step.

In 1955, Eddie was one of the preeminent street drug dealers in the county of Queens. I had the opportunity to accompany him to Harlem, along with two other guys, John and Lou, where Eddie "re-upped" (replenished his supply). Following the procurement, the four of us proceeded to my home in Polack Alley. As we sat at the kitchen table after injecting heroin, Dad appeared at the front door. The serene netherworld of "dopery" was quickly interrupted by a flurry of activity. Needles, cookers, eyedroppers, and dope disappeared. Lou had just finished wiping the blood from his arm when dad appeared in the room. "Hi boys." They replied, "Hi Mr. Gilbert."

The conversation drifted to a major topic of the day—the Emmett Till murder. Emmett Till, a 14-year-old African-American boy, was savagely beaten to death in Mississippi because of alleged inappropriate behavior toward a white woman. The mood of the guys was that justice prevailed in Mississippi. John proclaimed, "Those hillbillies sure know how to handle niggers," followed by laughter. I didn't quite see it that way but being a follower and having zero confidence in my own opinion, I nervously went along with the majority. The guys expected Dad to agree. However, Dad remarked that although the boy was ignorant of southern norms, he did not deserve what he got. He said that what happened to young Emmett was disgustingly evil and probably would go unpunished. Dad went on to explain that the world was 75 percent "colored," and that white folks were a minority but had managed to steal the resources and enslave much of the earth's nonwhite population for the past few centuries. And that "colored" folks, who are not stupid, as evidenced by their achievement in every human endeavor, would eventually assume their rightful place in world leadership. The good news, Dad explained, was that when "colored" people assumed leadership, they would not treat us as badly as we had treated them.

My silent reaction to this was typical. Why did Dad have to come out as a "nigger-lover" to my very important friends? I also felt a paradoxical sense of shame in realizing that I was quite possibly a closet "nigger-lover" myself. Still, I remained ignorant and fearful of my obligation to challenge racism.

Dad was born in a Cajun community somewhere in Louisiana in 1890. His first language was a variation of French mixed with English. His parents (my paternal grandparents), Elijah Jay Gilbert and Claire La Mare, divorced when Dad was a young child. Dad and his mom then moved to Crystal Falls, Michigan, to live with his Mom's parents (my great-grandparents).

Dad had very fond memories of his grandparents. His grandpa was a Civil War veteran who survived Andersonville, the Confederate prison where many Union soldiers perished. He described his grandpa as a robust, humorous man who would tell stories and sing songs about his experiences fighting the rebels, much to the chagrin of his wife, who admonished him for "teaching a young boy such terrible language." One of the ditties Dad remembered was: *In this prison hole I sit— Covered up with shit—With the shadow of my cock upon the ground*"—Dad laughed heartily in recalling this memory.

The Great-grandpa stories abound. "Ain't nobody gonna make me fight," a fellow draftee informed Great-grandpa before their induction. Great-grandpa's response: "Ain't nobody gonna make you fight; they just take you where the fighting is, and then you use your own judgment." Although opposed to slavery, Great-grandpa believed that morality had little to do with actual combat. According to Dad, Great-grandpa described combat as: "You kill folks based on the color of their uniform." He went on to imply that the only protectors you have are men whose uniform is the same color as yours; that patriotism and honor are absent in combat, replaced by a need for survival, which generates a strong bond among comrades in arms. Indeed, I have heard members of Veterans for Peace witness a need to return to Iraq or Afghanistan for additional deployment to stand shoulder to shoulder with their comrades who were in danger.

"If the world is to survive, governments will have to devise another method of addressing conflict." Although these words, coming from Great-grandpa, appear painfully ironic in the 21st century (50 million deaths from World War ll alone as opposed to one million from the Civil War), I repeated them to my sons. In return, they will be repeated to my grandchildren and will contribute to keeping the movement for peace alive.

Dad had little formal education. As a teenager, he was kicked out of Catholic school for raising a troubling question. In one class, he learned that God created Adam and Eve and the entire world in six days, about 6,000 years ago. In another class, he learned about a rock that was 50,000 years old. He wanted to know, "Who made the rock?" I'm sure that this question was just the tip of an iceberg that led to his departure, as he was a natural-born skeptic.

Dad was not allowed in Aunt Mary's home. I don't know exactly why, but his free-spirited humor and iconoclastic outlook on life were a direct contradiction to the religious rigidity practiced in the house of Uncle Joe. Dad hated Uncle Joe. My earliest memory of Dad was at about the age of 14 when I moved to the O'Donnell's. Initially, I felt quite uncomfortable. He didn't talk like people in Brooklyn, and I was often embarrassed by his openness with people. He would talk to anybody—in stores, elevators, parks—complete strangers. Despite his quirky behavior, people usually had nice things to say about him; he was well-liked. After the family reunited in Polack Alley, I got to know him and initially discovered that he was an interesting and very smart man. However, as my character flaws multiplied, I found him to be a convenient excuse for my problems, whether I was on the street or locked up.

Following the release from the Peanut Farm in 1966, I returned to Chicago and got a bartender's job at the Front Page, a place that featured drag queen shows. The Front Page had mob ties, catered to gays, lesbians, and prostitutes, both male and female, and a variety of drugs were available. Thus, I picked up where I left off, still clueless, and doing the same things that got me locked up in the first place. I met Jackie there and had a relationship with her that lasted over a year. Jackie was a good person, but, like me, she was broken.

Originally from Appalachia, she lived in poverty for the first decade of her life. When she was 10, her father, in a drunken rage, set fire to the family's trailer home, killing her two younger brothers and her dog. Jackie and her mom survived while her dad was executed for the murders. Shortly afterward, Jackie's mom married a physician who provided a means for Jackie and her mom to escape poverty. However, this stepdad turned out to be a sexual predator who repeatedly subjected Jackie to abuse. After unsuccessfully attempting to convince her mom of these attacks, Jackie left home in her mid-teens, with an increased absorption in alcohol, drugs, promiscuous sex, and eventual prostitution, leading to an inevitable geographic cure to Chicago.

Although I successfully maintained employment at the Front Page for about a year, my drug-addled behavior caught up with me, and I lost the job. That's when my life deteriorated into domestic violence, frequent moves to avoid paying rent, and eventual homelessness. I spent many nights in a 25-cent flophouse.

I remember one bright sunny morning leaving the flophouse and looking at a billboard advertisement that stated, "There's a Ford in your future." In a moment of clarity, I thought to myself, "Ain't no Ford in my future." I started crying, not out of my usual self-pity but as a realization of the utter hopelessness of my life and the mess I had made of it. This fleeting moment of self-awareness dissipated in the dubious pursuit of intoxication.

At the same time, I engaged in the ultimate result of victim-blaming—severe verbal abuse and assaultive behavior toward my only friend, Jackie. Referring to her past associations with black men, I called her a "nigger-lover." I made a derogatory reference to the sexual abuse that she experienced as a young girl, saying, "I know that you initiated the sex with your stepfather." Jackie was not a passive recipient of this abuse, so our confrontations were monumental, but we invariably made up, crying in each other's arms.

As time went on, I began to see the handwriting on the wall. Given my lack of success in maintaining a stable existence, I believed that another trip to the penitentiary was inevitable, so I "booked." I left Jackie stranded alone in Chicago and arrived in New York in similar circumstances as on my return from California—broke and raggedy. And again, Mom came to the rescue. I recall feeling a sense of relief, not the least concerned about Jackie; I had no remorse until later in life.

Since Dad had passed and my sister Ann was safe in the convent, Mom gave up the home in Polack Alley and moved back into employee housing at Creedmoor State Hospital where she worked. Having started at Creedmoor in 1938 as a clerk, she went on to become an office manager. Creedmoor State Hospital is a 40-building complex situated on a campus in Queens Village that had historically provided residential treatment for the mentally ill. Mom worked there for 35 years and enjoyed a very favorable reputation. She was considered a loyal friend and strong union supporter by many of her coworkers, and a reliable, conscientious worker by supervisors.

"We are strong people, Jimmy; our peasant farmer forbearers provided nourishment and modeled a work ethic that contributed greatly to human development. We overcome adversity. We don't give up. I pray that you will stop saturating your mind and spirit with the poison that you have injected into your body, as I am confident that your many God-given qualities will expel the demons that have entered your soul.

As long as I have breath, I will encourage your incredible potential and never abandon you." These words are from a letter that I received from Mom while incarcerated. To this day, they offer comfort from the "cringe moments" of guilt and shame that I continue to experience when I think of what I put my mom through.

Mom had no difficulty getting me a job at Creedmoor, which included employee room and board. By moving into a furnished room in D building, where I shared residence with other male workers, I got a reprieve from the self-destructive and, at times, dangerous life in Chicago. Most of my fellow residents in D building were African-American, and I felt at home, enjoying companionship and a shared interest in jazz. However, I almost immediately gravitated toward drug users, and there were more than several. Thus, I continued the "broken record" element of my existence—employing failed solutions to life's problems and expecting different results.

The Yard Department job at Creedmoor provided much satisfaction, despite a sustained ignorance about the need to address my substance abuse. I was introduced to ground maintenance, which included spring planting, giant tree pruning, lawn maintenance for the doctors' cottages, Christmas decorations, leaf removal, and snow removal. Snow removal was particularly significant. Snowfall exceeding two inches defined an emergency, and all Yard Department workers were required to report to work during this regardless of the time of day or the day of the week. Clearing snow from the hospital grounds during a blizzard made me feel like one of the guys with the white hats, coming to the rescue.

Indeed, my overall experience in the Yard Department, for the first time in my life, led to a feeling that I was doing something important. In retrospect, I realize that although I liked my work, the progression of my addiction made it impossible to establish genuine connections with other people. I had no friends. I did manage to last two years as a Creedmoor employee until my addictive illness completely took over, resulting in deteriorating job performance, unreliability, and frequent altercations culminating in arrest and incarceration. This, however, became the beginning of a turning point.

In 1967, following an arrest for possession, I was mandated to three years at NACC, the New York State Narcotic Addiction Control Commission. This entailed one year in residential confinement and two on parole, where support services were available, and continued freedom was contingent on remaining drug-free. NACC was the product of an enlightened time in history; its principal goal was to transition the paradigm of addiction from a criminal problem to a social problem. It began in the mid-1960s and lasted until the early 1970s.

History records NACC as an unsuccessful attempt to address the drug problem in the United States. The safety nets like NACC were controlled by the government and put in place like patchwork, and they were not comprehensive enough to meet the need. But they existed! There have been many societal advances since the '60s, but conservative attacks have weakened protections and have almost eliminated the few existing safety nets. If these safety nets had not existed in the 1960s, I would still be a high school dropout. At present, getting a GED while incarcerated is next to impossible and public college tuitions are unaffordable for low income people.

In the 1950s, the standard of living for the American working class was among the highest in the world (paradoxically within a Jim Crow nation). And by the 1960s, the civil rights movement had gained enough momentum to shut down Jim Crow, and in its aftermath, provided a climate for the eventual establishment of programs like NACC. Concurrently, the United States began losing ground to Japan, Western Europe,

Taiwan, and other burgeoning capitalist countries in competition for world markets. In their quest for profit, capitalists in the U.S. developed a strategy of deindustrialization and capital mobility as corporations moved industry to countries without labor laws. In this process, unemployment increased dramatically while underemployment began its ubiquitous ascent, especially in communities of color. This signaled the beginning of the deterioration of the American working class and, eventually, the American middle class. Good jobs, like Joe Flaherty's dad had, disappeared. Historically, unemployment was correlated with increased addiction, crime, and incarceration, so scapegoats were needed. As race, addiction, and crime became interwoven, NACC, and other safety-net entities disappeared. All the while, many U.S. citizens remained clueless regarding this gradual deterioration.

I arrived at Mid-Hudson, a NACC facility, full of obligatory resentment and self-pity. I don't recall exactly when this attitude began to dissipate but dissipate it did. This was a time of heightened political unrest related to the Vietnam War, African-American community uprisings, an energized Women's Movement and South African apartheid. I began hearing statements like,"If you're not part of the solution, you're part of the problem." I no longer wanted to be considered a problem, and, for the first time, I experienced hope. Marathon group therapy sessions provided firm bedrock for self-examination while a literature class familiarized me with Erich Fromm, Karl Marx, Joseph Conrad, Balzac, and other literary luminaries. As I earned a GED, I was beginning to leave the narrow world in which I existed and enter the world of the living. This was the meager beginnings of what ultimately became a lifetime adventure.

NACC, being a part of the New York criminal justice system, maintained racial segregation. Marathon therapy was divided into three segments—black, white, and "Spanish." The brothers elected to use their marathon time to study the Koran. Those who were more interested in psychotherapy were generally accepted in the "Spanish" group while the white group maintained racial homogeneity. However, educational activities could not be segregated. As a result, there wasn't the same tension between the races at Mid-Hudson that existed in traditional jailhouse communities. In looking back, I realize that segregation was the norm. The United States was fundamentally a Jim Crow nation. The North could always point to the South as the land of bigotry while implicitly denying fundamental opportunities to black folks. Until recently, with rare exceptions, African-Americans could not move into a white community anywhere in America, so why would a bunch of dopefiends practice racial inclusion?

A principal factor in my attitude change at Mid-Hudson was an inadvertent stand against racism. I use the term "inadvertent" because I did not take this stand to challenge racism, but rather in response to what I believed was an attack on a victim without power. The entire population of Mid-Hudson lived on three floors, each floor divided into three components, each component divided into ten six-man rooms. The rooms were further categorized along racial lines—black, white, and "Spanish." When a new inmate arrived from the two-week quarantine, he reported to his assigned destination based on his race.

One day, following the arrival of a new inmate, a correction officer decided to play a joke and sent an 18-year-old black kid, to a white room that four inmates and I occupied. The kid, appearing uneasy, sat on the empty bed. Almost immediately, the taunting began. A dopefiend, Billy March, began chanting menacingly, "Afro! Afro! Afro!" and was accompanied by snickers. The kid became visibly upset, and I thought to myself, "He's just a kid, this ain't right." I approached the kid, put my hand on his shoulder, and said, "Come with me."

Billy March was blocking the room entrance, and as I approached, I said: "Get the fuck out of my way March, anybody wants to mess with this kid gotta go through me first." At that time, I was bench pressing 300 pounds, and although small in height, I was big in body. Anyway, I wasn't worried about Billy March; he was a loudmouth punk. I was concerned about a guy named Joey Falco, who was a killer and a racist. I looked at Joey as I exited with the kid. He stared me down but didn't make a move. I breathed a sigh of relief and brought the kid to his people.

The reaction to this incident was unusual. The diehard racists reacted predictably; some ignoramus from Brooklyn remarked, "Why'd you get involved with the 'yoms?' That wasn't very smart," while Joey Falco, fortunately, hid his displeasure. For the most part, I gained overall respect. Although the reaction from most of the white guys was one of indifference, several of the black and "Spanish" guys exhibited warmth that I never expected, leading to a friendship with Juan Morales.

Juan was a budding writer and poet whose interest in politics and literature complemented my newfound discoveries. After my release from Mid-Hudson, we maintained contact for a few months, but after losing touch, I got word that Juan had died from an overdose—another heart-wrenching example of the devastating power of addiction.

I was released from Mid-Hudson in the spring of 1969. I was 33 years old, and for the first time after being released from an institution, did not immediately head for a cop spot or a liquor store. The move toward doing the right thing convinced me that I could have friends who were not lowlifes. This was indeed a new beginning, and I will always be grateful to NACC.

5. DISCOVERY

Since I owed the state of New York two years, I was assigned to a Narcotic Parole Officer, a guy by the name of Gene Tice. Gene, a remarkable man, pulled me into a safety net. He encouraged gainful employment and provided "how-to" advice in negotiating the job market, which led to a good job at the Jamaica Water Company in Queens. The application papers at Jamaica Water Company did not include a "box" to be checked regarding past criminal activity. If under similar circumstances, I had applied for a job in the 21st century, the "box" would have deemed me ineligible, another example of an absence of hope and opportunity that exists now.

At the Water Company, I found much satisfaction in learning the rudiments of water main installation and repair and envisioned a promising career with eventual promotions to foreman and even inspector. I felt at ease with working guys while experiencing fear of more educated citizens. In challenging this fear and mistrust, Gene Tice insisted that I was college material and maintained that I needed to enroll at the Borough of Manhattan Community College as quickly as possible, advising that I was eligible under open enrollment. I was 33 years old at the time, attempting to negotiate the real world with an abundance of guilt and shame from a wasted life. Consequently, I questioned whether I belonged in college, but Gene would accept no hesitation and went on to assure me that college was the right place for me.

Gene is gone now; he passed sometime in the early 1980s. He was a peace officer who carried a weapon but remained an unapologetic liberal. I never got to know much about his background and family life, but in my memory, Gene remains a surrogate older brother who always provided good direction. Utilizing Gene's guidance as a compass to reroute my life, I went on to matriculate at BMCC.

I remember attending my first class, a summer course in Psychology 101, and feeling like a fish out of water among a group of intelligent young people. I thought, "None of these people talk like me, and I have nothing in common with them." I was batting 1,000 at failure and was concerned that I was in over my head. I had no confidence in my ability to contribute to class discussions. I sat in silence, took copious notes, and spent an inordinate amount of time studying—until I got the results of the mid-term exam—an "A" with encouraging praise from the instructor. From the second half of the semester on, I didn't shut up, expressing thoughts with a growing certitude. I didn't begin to acknowledge the importance of humility until later in life. Nevertheless, I went on to experience a lot of satisfaction from my time at BMCC.

It was at BMCC that I met Fredda, my first intimate adult relationship that wasn't fueled by drugs or alcohol. Our first date started with personal tension. I thought, "what if she discovers that I'm a lowlife pretending to be normal?" Somehow, I managed to express that I was not used to associating with normal people and apologized if my behavior appeared incorrect. What Fredda shared with me erased the discomfort level and initiated several hours of exchanging revealing history.

Fredda was raised with an older brother and two younger sisters. When she was 10, her mom went into a deep depression that lasted over six years, and she spent most of her days wearing a nightgown. The withdrawal of parental love, coupled with adult responsibilities for her younger sisters, left her in a state of uncertainty and mistrust. Wiping a tear from her eye, she confided: "My dad and my brother weren't much help at that time; I was lost." Fredda, the over-burdened child, left home in her late teens, rejected college, and went on to several failed relationships and other disappointments. Like me, Fredda was attempting to put her life back together. Following a couple of years in psychotherapy, she gained confidence in herself, and her relationship with her family improved dramatically. Fredda's disclosure prompted me to acknowledge for the first time that I felt "less than" but wanted to be normal. This level of sharing was new to me.

At that time, Fredda was in treatment with Lisa Friedman, a psychologist whose emphasis was mainly on group psychotherapy. I began treatment with Lisa in the summer of 1969. During my initial session, I requested group therapy, but Lisa believed I was too fragile and required individual work first. I was taken aback. I knew that I was a dopefiend, an ex-con, and a thief, but fragile was insulting. Nevertheless, I experienced Lisa as a knowledgeable and powerful person and did not challenge her. After two months, she put me in a group which, for me, was a major accomplishment.

Initially, Lisa's group provided rudimentary instruction on how to behave among non-criminals. More importantly, treatment with Lisa greatly reinforced my curiosity about the world, a move that established alternatives to self-pity, grandiosity, and a lack of empathic concern for others. Lisa suggested that I go to an anti-war demonstration in Washington. I responded, "Why do I have to go to Washington?" She replied, "Because that's where the good people are."

I remember declaring, "When I walked into Dr. Lisa Friedman's office for the first time, the sun shone on me." Lisa demonstrated the importance of service in the path to peace. She advised that I reduce "taking" and increase "giving. Go where the good people are and try to make the world a better place."

Shortly after starting treatment with Lisa, I moved in with Fredda and her Shetland sheepdog, Lady. Together, we pursued a sustained interest in education and the peace movement. I also resumed a long-lost interest in sports. Mike Kaufman, a popular sportswriter for the left press, became a paradigm in my transition to adult male-hood. Together with Mike Glick, Mike Sussman, Steve Kramer, Dominick Faraguna, Jim Noonan, Ken Segal, and many from the peace movement, I began lifetime friendships that provided examples of what it is to be a grown-up. For the first time in a very long time, I had real friends.

Mike Kaufman and I often went to the 96th Street courts for blackball, while weekend softball and pick-up basketball often included women. I can honestly say that throughout this period, from 1969 until 1972, I had no conscious desire for drugs or alcohol. Consequently, I thought that I was cured—an ex-dopefiend—but I was in for a tragic awakening.

In 1969, the student body at BMCC, in keeping with the political climate on college campuses, elected a variety of radicals and renamed the student government—*The Third World Coalition*. Because of the newly acquired open enrollment, which provided higher education opportunities for people previously shut out of the system, BMCC became home to many students who had children and jobs. Childcare, therefore, was a necessity. Faced with this problem, BMCC's director dismissed it, stating that it was not the responsibility of colleges to provide "babysitting" services to its students. The Third World Coalition found this unacceptable and organized a student strike.

Amid shouts of "on strike, shut it down," classrooms emptied, and the school shut down with a picket line outside. The director was not happy. He took photographs of coalition leaders and strikers, called the police, and demanded criminal charges. I was helping to empty classrooms when the police arrived. I suddenly realized that I was on parole, and even a disorderly conduct or trespassing charge could jeopardize my freedom. I hid in a broom closet where I found a custodial uniform shirt that I could squeeze into even though it was much too small for me. Although several of my fellow strikers got arrested, I emerged with a push broom and swept the hallway, which prevented my arrest. Ultimately, no one was convicted, and the strike ended in a student victory. BMCC established childcare, which solidified my identification with progressive politics.

As time went on, the water company job generated a conflict. I was working with white working guys most of whom leaned toward social conservativism, while I was practicing my newly found progressivism. Some of the guys thought I was weird in that I didn't drink and went to peace demonstrations. However, I got along with most of them and felt included. Here is a story that I wrote for a creative writing class during the spring of 1970:

It's Friday, 5:30 am. Although dressed, I'm not ready to leave for work yet, having just poured my first cup of freeze-dried coffee while listening to AM radio, which informs that there is a good chance of rain. I like summer rain. I like it better when it starts to rain heavily before 7:30 am, and work is suspended. Dealer's choice poker in the back of the shed is a wonderful diversion from digging up streets. But it will probably start raining before the job is half-finished, necessitating working in the rain and getting wet and muddier than usual. Wet and muddy are not really that bad, what is terribly annoying is the fact that things become uncertain and confusing when you work in the rain, sort of like trying to function in a mass of grey Jell-O.

I remember one night last winter, when, as part of an emergency crew, I was helping repair a water main during a heavy rainstorm. There were six of us, me, and five guys whom I secretly viewed with moral superiority. They supported the debacle in Vietnam, and the Nixon creep who was prosecuting it—"working-class sellouts," I concluded. Anyway, the six of us dug a trench, exposed the broken main, and began the process of repair. It was very cold, and you could see the direction of the wind and rain reflected in the glare of emergency lights that we strung up over the area. The canvas lean-to covering the lead pot that was sitting on a burner gave one a vision of a macabre picnic attended by hooded demons, their bodies hidden by glistening yellow rain gear.

"The pump stopped," shouted one of the demons, "somebody get the motherfucker started before we drown." A few minutes prior to this, our two-way radio produced its last angry burst of static and died. This was a bad situation. It was the temperature of the witches tit with the water level gradually ascending to the area of the testicles. Six guys huddled in raingear with half a repaired water main and its branches of pipe exposed in a trench, sort of a Rube Goldberg nightmare. Some of us frantically bailed water while the others worked on the broken main. Somehow, we finished the job. The payloader pushed the icy mud back into the hole. We erected barricades and hung lanterns. We then went to a warm saloon where we cursed the company, the bosses, the radio, and the pump. We laughed and joked in the manner of working-class self-deprecation. The collective mood was victorious.

A few weeks later, I passed by the spot where we were working, which, by this time, the road repair crew had transformed into a patch on the road. I felt like a soldier returning to the scene of a major battle which somehow will never be forgotten—God bless a working man!

Unfortunately, life wasn't always infused with working-class comradery at the water company. There was political conflict. The American flag, for many, symbolized blind patriotism and antagonism toward those who questioned the "righteousness" of America's participation in the war. This attitude was reflected in the obligatory presence of American flags on Jamaica Water Company trucks. I worked on a truck with Vinnie, a Vietnam veteran, and Joe, our immediate supervisor. In an attempt at equal representation, I chalked peace signs on the back of our truck, which were promptly erased by Vinnie. I was furious. I wanted to burn all the flags on the 10-15 trucks belonging to the company. Common sense prevailed, however. Joe's sentiments were with Vinnie, but we dealt with this conflict in a good-natured manner, mutually respecting each other's ability to work together.

Political conflict at the water company climaxed following the Kent State Massacre. Kent State was the scene of an anti-war protest in which thirteen students were gunned down by the National Guard. Four died. Though many reacted to the tragedy at Kent State with shock and grief, it heightened the fierce polarization of what was the Vietnam era. The morning following the attack, we had breakfast at our usual stop—Vinnie, Joe, and me. Joe had a copy of the *Daily News*, which depicted the massacre on its front page. He remarked, "Four fuckin' Jews. They got what they deserved."

Blinded by rage and screaming hysterically, I went after Joe. Vinnie and other water company workers who were in the coffee shop, restrained me until I began to calm. Joe apologized, and we continued to work together, but our relationship was never the same. Vinnie, however, painted a peace sign on the back of our truck, exclaiming, "This truck respects all opinions!" In September 1970, President Nixon's Commission on Campus Unrest concluded that "the indiscriminate firing of rifles at a crowd of (Kent State) students and the deaths that followed were unnecessary, unwarranted, and inexcusable."

The end of this episode marked a critical turning point in my life. Through the influence of Gene Tice, I was offered a job at the Narcotic Addiction Control Commission as a "Narcotic Aide," sort of an assistant counselor. I left the water company for NACC, which offered a flexible schedule so that I could attend school fulltime. And so began a fulfilling career and my life's calling in the profession of social work.

Healthcare was different in those days, less rigid and

friendlier in great part because of the absence of the current managed care. I took part in a team of former addicts, social workers, a psychologist, and an administrator in the development of an innovative residential drug treatment program that ultimately lasted several years with much success. The program targeted clients who appeared motivated and required lower levels of custodial care than upstate facility mandates. We drew our population from NACC facilities throughout the state. Each treatment rotation was twelve weeks. Upon graduation, clients were required to complete a three-year commitment in paroled aftercare. The program itself had a low recidivism rate, and it was a rare occurrence when a client had to return to an upstate facility.

Although program activity included individual counseling, it centered mainly on group therapy and multi-family therapy in addition to a variety of classroom activities, including GED preparation. Also, weightlifting, basketball, and yoga were popular activities. Our yoga program had its origins during a lunchtime stroll on East 8th Street when a coworker and I came across a yoga establishment. We identified ourselves and inquired about the possibility of bringing yoga to our facility. The yoga folks welcomed the idea with enthusiasm. They were interested in conveying a message and method of attaining health, personal peace, and tranquility—sort of an antithesis to the big-shot-ism commonly associated with addiction.

Shortly after this meeting, our yoga program began in earnest with daily yoga classes starting at 7:30 am. These classes became so popular that we had to move them from a classroom to the gym to accommodate all the participants. Classes began with a sun salutation, an ancient Hindu practice that awakens involuntary organs and stretches every major muscle group in the body. After a lifetime of physical activity that included marathon competition, old age permits only walking on the treadmill. However, the one thing that has stayed with me all these years is that I still start my day with the sun salutation.

The creative writing class at BMCC inspired the beginnings of a therapy group based on free-associative writing. Participants were encouraged to write anything that came to mind and, if willing to face feedback, share it with the group. At first, there was hesitancy. Only a few group members shared their written material with the group. However, as time went on, discussions intensified, and fear diminished. Participants began to experience the group as a safe place that offered an opportunity for healing.

What a stark contrast to the preoccupation with behaviorism that dominates 21st-century mental health treatment where managed care mandates measurable goals and objectives. Such treatment-plan nonsense as "Johnny will smile at least once a day for the next week" is now replacing relationship-building. Here is an example of past relational work in a young man's initial attempt to break through a wall of isolation and mistrust: *I'm a grown-up! I'm twenty-four years old, and I have a man-sized dick. But I never had a real job. I'm smart, but I never got an education. I probably would have done better if I was white, but I don't like most white people anyway. Who the fuck am I?*

I lost contact with this young man, but he revealed in our last conversation that he planned to complete his GED and pursue training as an electrician. In retrospect, I believe that there is a relationship between his experience in the group and his subsequent ability to envision positive and realistic goals. This experience sparked my lifelong belief in people power: The power of a mutually supportive group to heal.

In 1971, while continuing to work for NACC, I graduated from BMCC with an associate degree and went on to take advantage of the new CUNY BA program. This program, a product of progressive thought, provided college credits for life experience and the ability to attend any of the seventeen New York City colleges. In addition to my degree, I was awarded 23 credits for life experience. I was able to attend classes in proximity to my workplace, yet another example of opportunities that have disappeared in the 21st century.

Lisa's groups led to a profound discovery—that the entire world wasn't what I imagined—an unforgiving and dangerous place. As a result of good people coming into my life, my world changed. I experienced a "spiritual awakening" with the startling realization that the whole world wasn't "full o' shit." Even so, I still didn't have a clue about alcoholism.

6. ALCOHOL, THE RAPACIOUS CREDITOR

After I completed my bachelor's degree at CUNY in 1973, I entered a downward spiral of alcohol relapse. I was politically active in the Freedom and Peace Party in addition to school and work, and my life became increasingly stressful. I believed that I was cured of my addiction and entertained the notion that alcohol was not a drug. I hadn't been drinking for three years, and my life had improved dramatically; therefore, there wasn't a problem. I reduced the current stress with an occasional airplane nip of whiskey—terrible decision! Within a short time, the airplane nip surged to a quart of vodka a day. The good news was that I was at the tail-end of my last college semester, and I'd managed to graduate with a 3.95 GPA before the serious progression set in, and the bottom fell out.

My alcoholism progressed with an accompanying reawakening of character flaws. As I continued to "sneak drink," Fredda could not tolerate the lies, broken promises, and erratic behavior that followed. She had no choice but to end the relationship. I sincerely believed that the relationship demise was her fault. In retrospect, the breakup with Fredda reinforces my present-day conviction that substance dependence gradually crushes spiritual energy and impacts all human contact. Once more, I was incapable of experiencing empathy, and satisfying immediate needs was my sole preoccupation. Grandiosity reared its ugly head, fueled by wounded pride and growing resentment. I believed that being an ex-dopefiend with a college degree were the ingredients for greatness. Under duress, I left NACC in search of a leadership position. I landed a job at Reality House, a drug treatment therapeutic community in Harlem. It lasted five days.

After drinking a quart of vodka the previous night, I attempted to lead an encounter group the following morning. Encounter groups or "attack therapy" were popular methods to treat addiction. The idea was to break down grandiosity, self-pity, and immaturity by direct confrontation—prior to supportive gestures. This method provided enlightenment to many addicts with personality disorders (although it could present a danger to those addicts with psychosis). Nevertheless, the Reality House clients saw through my pretense of being in control, and attacked, electing to use suspicion of my drinking as a topic. I insisted on my moral superiority while vehemently denying excessive alcohol consumption, but I was painfully unsuccessful. The group ended on a rather somber note, and my employment ended in alcohol-related disgrace.

Meanwhile, Fredda went on to complete graduate school and began a very successful career in social work, specializing in addiction treatment. Years later, sober and practicing AA's amends principle, I had amicable and meaningful contact with Fredda before her passing at the age of 60. A lifelong smoker, she died from a severe asthma attack. Like AA's co-founder, Bill Wilson, Fredda helped many addicts find a way out of their addiction but could not overcome her own addiction to nicotine. I delivered a eulogy at her memorial service.

My alcoholism steadily progressed after the Reality House episode, but the real possibility of homelessness, prison, and permanent un-employability prevented drug use. However, I remained clueless about my dangerous downward spiral. I had lost two jobs and my relationship with Fredda since returning to drinking. Still, the powerful reappearance of self-pity and grandiosity provided a defensive barrier, keeping me from admitting personal difficulties and seeking help. During this period of relapse from 1972 to 1976, I stayed in treatment with Lisa Friedman and minimized my drinking problem. In those days, most mental health treatment providers, including Lisa Friedman, didn't have a clue about alcoholism. When I received $50,000 from Mom's union death benefit in 1974, I was in the throes of alcohol relapse. Lisa knew that my drinking was a problem and attempted a few interventions that included controlled drinking and Antabuse, but the progression of the illness took hold. Neither Lisa nor I considered AA. (Following my entrance into AA, Lisa did some research on AA and became an enthusiastic supporter of meeting attendance, despite her limited experience in alcoholism treatment.)

When the inheritance arrived, Lisa knew my impulsivity would lead to wasting that money. Therefore, she became my designated payee, meaning that withdrawals exceeding one-hundred dollars had to be co-signed by her. She was quite amenable to outlays of funds for stereo equipment and clothes, but put her foot down when I considered lending $5,000 to a "friend." Consequently, when I was sober in 1977, my future wife and I were able to purchase a home in Teaneck. I'm sure that I would have messed up that money if Lisa Friedman hadn't blatantly violated patient-therapist boundaries by taking charge of my finances.

Lisa passed in 2001. In presenting a eulogy at her memorial service, I referred to Lisa as one who brought people together, a friendship organizer, and a matchmaker. I asked those whose lifetime partnerships began in one of Lisa's groups to identify themselves. Many raised their hands. I asked those who acquired lifetime friendships because of Lisa's groups to identify themselves, and many more hands were raised. After the service, the rabbi informed me that "matchmaking" is a mitzvah in the Jewish culture, and clearly one of Lisa Friedman's greatest gifts to all of those who had the good fortune to work with her.

Following the Reality House debacle, I got a counselor's job at the city methadone program. Although alcoholism is common among methadone clients, my caseload had few alcoholics, perhaps because I only recognized alcoholism in those who drank more than me. In retrospect, I was increasingly unreliable and, at times, unpredictable.

While attempting to maintain a semblance of order in my life, alcohol dependency ultimately prevailed. One Friday night in early 1973, I left an after-work party in a semi-inebriated state and decided since my life was a mess anyway; I might as well enjoy some dry goods. I went to a cop spot, purchased valium and a five-dollar bag of heroin, and went home where I consumed the purchased product—and overdosed. Twelve hours later, when I woke up, I was not able to move my left arm or my left leg. The medical term for this condition is called the Crush syndrome, which is when prolonged nerve pressure and lack of movement cause severe swelling and paralysis. I managed to crawl to a neighbor's apartment and got him to call my friend, Mike Sussman, who arranged for an ambulance to take me to Columbia Presbyterian Hospital.

That was a low point. Although I stayed out of jail throughout the relapse, the return to a drinking life activated my character flaws and resulted in the overdose and hospitalization. I was terrified. I went back to, "Ain't no Ford in my future." Paradoxically, I found a healing community of friends while in the hospital.

At Columbia Presbyterian, I spent a week in intensive care and four months in a rehab ward called Neuro Eight, where I received a steady stream of visitors. There were times when as many as ten people waited to visit me. Although still self-absorbed, for the first time in my adult life, I had real friends. There was Mindy Thompson (now Mindy Thompson Fullilove), Mike Kaufman, Mike Glick, Sonia Ivany, Dominick Faraguna, Alan and Beverly Lefkowitz, Ben and Alice Spivack, Steve and Loren Kramer, JJ Johnson, Florence Barnes, Jim Noonan, and numerous others, many of whom I continue to have close, meaningful contact with today. I fully realize now that replacing dopefiends and criminals with these wonderful people brought rays of sunshine, hope, and optimism into my life.

They more than proved their value in July of 1973, when Mom passed. Mom had always been my anchor. After her death, I went into a severe depression and greatly needed the ministering of a healing community of people. I lost the ability to converse—when somebody said "hello" to me, I'd fumble for an answer. During one of her frequent visits, Mindy sat in silence and held my hand, which made me feel protected and safe. One Saturday morning, Mindy appeared accompanied by a young woman who she introduced as Ilene. Little did I know that Ilene would become my best friend and my life's companion.

I also had the good fortune of being under the care of Dr. Raphael Levine, a resident who conducted my treatment in a no-nonsense manner, insisting that I keep my leg brace on and engage in all recommended exercises even when I didn't feel like it. He was unimpressed when I informed him that I was a "Senior Rehabilitation Counselor" in a New York City drug treatment program. He remarked that if I wanted to waste my life, that was my business. But as his patient, he would do all he could to sustain my physical recovery. He did just that!

Because of the nonstop swelling associated with Crush syndrome, Dr. Levine had to do a "cut down" procedure shortly after my admission, which involved cutting into my left arm and leg to relieve the pressure. The procedure was successful in that the swelling stopped. However, several days later, when returning from X-Ray, I was on a gurney in a hallway when Dr. Levine passed by. He did a quick observation and bent to examine my leg while instructing the attendant to "move this patient to a treatment room immediately." Dr. Levine discovered an infection that would have resulted in an amputation had he not acted quickly. A nurse informed me later that Dr. Levine had indeed saved my left leg.

In the summer of 1973, shortly after Mom's funeral, I had

been discharged from Neuro Eight, returned to work at the methadone program, and resumed drinking. Mom's funeral provided an opportunity to reconnect with Aunt Mary after many years. The last contact that I had with her was a phone conversation in 1974. I was in the throes of active alcoholism and fighting old battles; I was angry. Aunt Mary asked, "How's your love life?" I remember, as a youngster, hearing, and "It's just as easy to fall in love with a Catholic as it is with a Protestant." This rule emphasized the importance of marrying Catholics (Jews were not even a consideration). Except for moving in with the O'Donnell's, I never directly challenged Aunt Mary, relying instead on familiar passive-aggressive ways of expressing anger. So I responded to her question about my "love life" by saying that I was keeping company with a woman (Ilene), "but she is not of our religion." "Oh," asked Aunt Mary, "what religion?" I responded like a dagger, "She's Jewish." Aunt Mary replied, "That's nice. You know, there's not too much difference between Jews and Poles. Remember when you were little, and we used to go to the Jewish dairy store for pot cheese and farmer's cheese? Remember when Grandma and Mrs. Rosenfield used to gossip in Polish? We have a lot more in common with the Jews than we do with the Italians, even though the Italians go to our church."

Aunt Mary had a remarkable way of defusing inner turmoil. My mood lightened, and the conversation switched to a recipe for pierogi. She was an excellent cook and never consulted a cookbook, measuring ingredients with a practiced eye. Her perogies remain a delicious memory of exquisite taste, but trying to explain her method of preparation over the phone was akin to attempting to explain how to tie shoelaces over the phone. I was never able to reproduce Aunt Mary's perogies, but her love remains.

After a couple of years, I fell into a routine that accommodated my active alcoholism. Knowing that as soon as I ingested alcohol, I would continue until I got drunk, I rarely drank publicly and ceased almost all political activity. Afraid of being found out, I drank alone. After work, I routinely stopped at the liquor store, got a quart of vodka, went next door to the bodega for two 16-ounce cans of beer, and went home to my apartment in Washington Heights. I would gulp down the vodka and beer, pass out, wake up to more vodka and pass out, repeating the process until morning. Many days, I had to look in the garbage to find out what I had eaten the previous night because I had blacked out. I managed to get to work most days, although in no shape to function adequately.

I did not drink during work, not even when there were celebrations, and it was acceptable. My coworkers would have a drink or two at these celebrations, but I fully realized that I didn't just drink, I got drunk. As the consequences of drinking increasingly eclipsed the short-lived pleasures of drinking, I entertained the goal of not drinking. But attempts to stop on my own led to a realization that I had no choice in the matter—I couldn't stop. At work, I was preoccupied with the coming evening's debauch, to the exclusion of almost all other thoughts and feelings. Isolation, terror, shame, and guilt prevailed. I eventually stopped going to work, and stayed home and drank until the intervention of Ilene, Mike Kaufman, and Mindy, who coordinated their efforts with two friends from the methadone program, Jim Noonan and Ken Segal. Jim and Ken then drove me to Freeport Hospital, one of the few facilities that provided alcoholism treatment in the New York metropolitan area.

Part Two

Here Comes The Sun

7. THE FELLOWSHIP

In March of 1976, at Freeport Hospital, I was introduced to the fellowship of Alcoholics Anonymous. Before becoming part of AA, misinformation and grandiosity informed my perception. I believed that as an addiction counselor with a history of drug treatment and psychotherapy, I was far too sophisticated to become involved in "boneyards," where a bunch of drunks told war stories and talked about God. However, when *my way* produced increasingly negative consequences, and I had nowhere else to go, I reconsidered—good decision! Since having "nowhere to go" included housing, Jim Noonan provided lodging in his home on Staten Island, where I began my journey with Alcoholics Anonymous. Although we haven't spoken in years, Jim has a permanent place on my gratitude list.

I immersed myself in AA meetings, and Ilene and I resumed our relationship. With Lisa Friedman's blessing, we established a household in Ilene's apartment in Washington Heights, along with our two cats, Jessica and Cinderella. At this time, Ilene and I decided to partner for life and planned a wedding for February 1977. Since she was a member of the Unitarian Universalist church in Montclair, New Jersey, the church provided accommodation for the wedding and reception. Ilene's family and all our friends joined us on a memorable and joyous occasion. Our friends and loved ones danced, sang, talked, and provided a veritable feast. My friend Susan said, "You had a real wedding, and your friends danced at your wedding." And that's when I started to have a glimpse of the way my life could be.

Ilene and I joined the Unitarian Universalist church in Paramus, New Jersey, sometime in the early 1980s. We became active members for 30 years, both serving on various committees and the Board of Trustees at different times, while my sons completed the Sunday school program. Ilene continues to be active in the church. I have great admiration for this community and their idea of "deeds, not creeds." Their historical commitment to social justice provided a spiritual home without demanding a belief in a supernatural being.

Meanwhile, I struggled with the "God" word that I frequently heard in AA meetings. Even though I considered the Twelve Steps or the AA principles of self-awareness and humility religious dogma, I felt safe in the AA rooms and realized that's where I needed to be. With time, AA's fellowship led me to the beginning of a lifetime search for enlightenment, despite what I perceived as the "religious trappings" in AA.

I never considered that not everyone *had* to agree with my point of view and that my point of view might not necessarily be the "right" one. This religious conflict metastasized into absurdity. Charley was an old friend I knew from the street and the jailhouse. I was quite pleased when we reconnected at an Upper West Side AA meeting. However, when Charley talked about his relationship with God since joining AA, I had to swallow my anger. I thought Charlie was a "stand-up guy" and a reliable comrade who would never betray a confidence. And now these AA religious fanatics were turning him into a born-again Protestant!

In 1976, all AA meetings ended with the Lord's Prayer from the Christian bible. I objected to this practice by not standing and looking annoyed while everyone else stood and recited the prayer. I'm sure a few attendees were offended, but invariably a few guys, led by Charley, would approach me with a handshake, a pat on the back, and a request to "keep coming back." I had enough street smarts to detect bullshit, and these drunks and dopefiends seemed for real. Ultimately, I wanted what they had, the God stuff notwithstanding; thus, the moral certitude began to wane.

When I first started to work on 149th Street, I was new to AA but felt safe and rejuvenated in AA meetings. Since the methadone clinic was often high-stress, I decided to find a lunchtime AA meeting and eventually joined a group just across the bridge in Harlem. The Harlem group is one of the oldest AA groups in New York City, having started as a "colored" group when de facto segregation was the rule. AA's *Big Book* documented personal stories in its early days that demonstrated efforts to challenge this cultural norm. A Jim Crow nation would not allow AA to integrate its activities. Still, literature, guidance, and financial help were provided to African-American groups by a variety of white AAs, including Bill Wilson. The first ongoing AA meeting on the East Coast took place in Wilson's home in Brooklyn.

There was *one* African-American member. To avoid serious confrontation with neighbors, Bill advised him to enter and exit through the side door of the house, so neighbors would assume that he was a "delivery boy." Once inside, he defied cultural norms. Following a history where African Americans were underrepresented, AA went on to become one of the most diverse organizations in the world. Step Eight in the *Twelve Steps and Twelve Traditions* professes that "Learning to live in the greatest peace, partnership, and brotherhood with all men and women, of whatever description, is a moving and fascinating adventure."

I was regularly attending the Harlem group when Ilene and I moved to New Jersey. Before the move, I had only gone to AA meetings on the Lower East Side, Harlem, the Bronx, and the West Side of Manhattan. I was shocked during my first New Jersey AA meeting by a sign that said, "This group does not approve of obscenities; please respect the wishes of the group." I hadn't expected how much more conservative suburban New Jersey was than New York City. I immediately caught a resentment. How do you get sober without cursing? Looking at all of the middle-class folks in that meeting, I thought to myself, "I'm probably the only one in this room who didn't vote for Richard Nixon."

The next day at the Harlem group, I sought out Norman to commiserate. Norman was an elderly guy whom I considered an AA scholar. I told him about the sign, implying that the people in New Jersey weren't doing it right. He said: "Tell you what you do—give them your permission to keep that sign." Norman went onto explain that if I "allowed" them to display that sign, it will impress them as to what a tolerant person I am, and he added, "It will make *you* feel better." After recovering from a long belly laugh, I began to realize that this was a powerful lesson, one that validates the Serenity Prayer — "Grant me the serenity to accept things that I cannot change." The Harlem group stands out in my memory as a place of love and wisdom. Ironically, that New Jersey group, of which I am still a member 40-plus later, has provided a lifetime of enduring friendship with many outstanding people.

I'd been in AA for ten years when I had the good fortune to witness Mike evolve from self-centeredness and isolation to a state of self-awareness while earning respect and forming friendships. When I first met Mike, everything annoyed him, and he let everybody know about it. Paul, his sponsor, after years of sobriety, suddenly became wheelchair-bound. Following the initial shock of having a permanent disability, Paul went on to experience a sense of peace and contentment in fellowship. Mike learned from this man; the lesson was not academic. Paul *showed* Mike how to enjoy life, despite its challenges. In striving for self-awareness, Mike realized that it's hard to pay attention to the rest of the world when all of your energy is self-contained. Mike wasn't a very popular guy when he started AA, but he now has the respect and admiration of many friends.

Mike recently reminded me of a conversation that we had a few years ago. A group of young women from Spring House regularly attended our Tuesday meeting. Spring House is a women's residential community for homeless substance abusers, many of whom have recently re-entered the community after being in jail. At the time, they were mainly "low-bottom" folks who often spoke about their problems in living. This annoyed Mike. He said: "These girls think that this is group therapy." I suggested that he give them permission to do group therapy. If he allowed it, others would see him as a tolerant man. Mike laughed. He understood, and after a few years, went on to thank me for the direction. I explained that it wasn't an original thought, that I got it from Norman, who advised me to "allow" the New Jersey group to keep their sign many years ago. That's how fellowship works.

Father John and I attended the same AA meeting on the West Side of Manhattan. His friendship provided valuable life lessons. Following a few conversations in which I addressed him as "Father," he stated that in AA, we are all at eye level, that the essence of our mutuality prohibits hierarchical titles, so I should address him by his given name. Ironically, I wasn't comfortable with this, despite my problems with the church (the boy leaves the church, but the church doesn't leave the boy). Eventually, I was able to envision "John" as an AA brother—another drunk just like me.

In one of our phone conversations, I questioned the value of prayer and had some unkind things to say about the Catholic Church. I wasn't trying to start an argument; I just wanted John to know who I was. During that process, he became my teacher. He believed that prayer, although a significant part of religion, actually transcends religion and is a basis for communication. Prayer is talking, and meditation is listening. John explained that although speech can at times lead to hatred and discord, for the most part, talking presents an opportunity to seek communion with others, and authentic listening is analogous to allowing the mind to focus on communication. In listening to others, we are invited into their personhood. This lesson has proven to be invaluable.

Sonny was a gangbanger long before it became fashionable. Raised in poverty on the streets of Harlem, he combatted his alienation with alcohol, heroin, and criminal activity, culminating in a lengthy sentence in Attica following a manslaughter conviction. When released in 1975, he was acutely aware that he was a "predicated felon"—a repeat offender. That meant that the slightest infraction of his parole could result in a life sentence. Since he was a dopefiend and an alcoholic, a principal parole stipulation was AA attendance. Sonny, a free spirit, did not want to return to jail, so he went to AA.

When I met him, he'd been sober for a year. I was warned that "this guy is very angry and does not like white people." I wanted his friendship anyway because he epitomized "free spirit." Besides, Sonny was a jazz encyclopedia who could riff Coltrane solos verbatim. With the AA community as our refuge, we developed a deep friendship.

While Sonny and I were fishing on a party boat from City Island, he confided that prayer helped him diffuse his anger and asked if I prayed. I said that I was an atheist and "why the fuck should I pray?" He replied, "If you can't pray, *practice*. It works." Such advice from anyone else on the planet wouldn't have garnered a moment's thought. However, I had watched Sonny transform from a man consumed with anger and hatred to a man of peace and brotherhood. As his self-awareness increased, Sonny discovered a world of good people and claimed that prayer was an essential ingredient in this transformation. I had to give prayer serious thought, so I began to practice—and I still practice, 40 years later. Sonny is gone, but his spirit remains.

Alcoholics Anonymous dates its origin to 1935 in Akron,

Ohio, where Bill Wilson (co-founder and principal architect) found himself desperate for a drink after having abstained from alcohol for six months. He gave himself a choice: He could help himself to a drink or help another alcoholic. Bill met with Bob Smith (co-founder and known as "Dr. Bob"), who was also contemplating his next drink. Bob told Bill he only had ten minutes. The meeting lasted several hours as both men strongly identified with the other and realized that they could help each other in sobriety.

Within three years, AA's membership expanded to Akron, Cleveland, and New York. Eventually, their numbers reached 100 men and women who reined in the downward trajectory of their lives and experienced a joy in living. Since this was a trial-and-error beginning, people wondered how Bob and Bill got sober. So, Bill engaged AA's first hundred members to codify and document the journey to sobriety for future generations. Thus, the Twelve Steps were born. In the ensuing 80 years, this group of 100 grew to over two-million AA members in more than 150 countries throughout the world. To this day, the wording of the Twelve Steps remains unchanged, complete with archaic culturalisms. However, the Steps have become a document that provides a lifetime of study, interpretation, and guidance.

I would argue that AA is based on two major components: The first is fellowship, which is the power of the collective where optimism prevails, and shame evaporates. The fellowship is one where virtually every member, at some point in time, had gotten drunk and made an ass of themselves, yet manage to focus on respect and a genuine desire to help fellow sufferers. Fellowship initiates healing. The second component is "A Design for Living," as enumerated in the Twelve Steps. I believe that the Steps are subject to interpretation depending on culture and religious belief. Many AA's believe in a supernatural being who created the world and will provide direct assistance to life's problems if petitioned. However, a growing number of independent thinkers in AA believe God is a concept, not a being, and utilize the steps as a path to self-awareness without dogmatic belief. I continue to witness within this group.

Initially, I identified as an atheist and have since embraced agnosticism with a tendency toward pantheism. I remember a Unitarian Universalist preacher who displayed a yellow flower that he plucked from the early spring grass as he ascended the pulpit. "This is God," he said. I thought, "What the hell is this guy talking about?" I have since come to believe that we are all part of the same stuff, part of a creative spirit, part of an interdependent web, part of "God"—whatever that is.

In earlier years, I was focused on violent thoughts, rage, and fantasies that ended in moral victory. What I recognize now is that imagined narcissistic injuries led to senseless resentments, self-pity, and grandiosity. With consistent sobriety, I began to contemplate/pray on an almost daily basis, which provided a space to examine my character flaws and to express gratitude for the blessings of family and friends. The result was gradual, but palpable, and brought me newfound peace. I am not petitioning a supernatural male being who singlehandedly created the universe, has personal access to everyone's innermost thoughts, loves humans, and is omnipotent, and will interfere with the laws of nature on behalf of petitioners, but yet punishes sin and ignores oppression. My experience with prayer is one of self-examination and an expression of gratitude. With time and practice, I realize that prayer must have predated religion.

AA prompted my belief that humans strive to survive through mutuality, through helping each other. It has been postulated that interdependence among humans is an actual law that determines all societal constructs. My understanding is that God is a metaphor, a mystery, a concept rather than a being, and, at best, a verb and not a noun. I believe that humans invented God in their image and likeness; if dolphins had a god, he would look like a dolphin.

There is a deep sense of mutuality in AA meetings where the common thread is suffering. Optimism prevails because its members aspire to relieve the suffering of their fellows. The invention of God provided a means to serenity for many in the practice of religion. But within the diverse theological views and often contradictory beliefs among the world's religions, a resulting commonality produced an illusion that divine power is responsible for all social outcomes. I believe divine power is people power.

My relationship with AA's Twelve Steps went from a superficial desire to understand them to a critical and historical study. Once I was able to look beyond the painfully condescending and dated text in AA's, *Twelve Steps and Twelve Traditions,* I discovered profound wisdom and a design for living. For the past twenty years, I've been meeting with a group of AA's on Sunday mornings to read and discuss the steps. Each week, we read a specific step in rotating order. The discussions are never boring or redundant, leading me to believe that like scripture, the *Twelve and Twelve* is a living document.

My take: Step One - *We admitted that we were powerless over alcohol – that our lives had become unmanageable,* provides a bedrock for self-examination, and an admission of powerlessness over alcohol. Since the ingestion of alcohol results in the proliferation of character flaws, an alcoholic has little chance of character growth while actively drinking.

Step Two - *Came to believe that a power greater than ourselves could restore us to sanity,* affirms that the quality of decision-making in the life of an active alcoholic is perhaps on the level of a young child—consequently, the need for the help of "another" power. I never had a problem with AA's

Second Step. It was quite evident that my way of dealing with alcohol and drugs was not working. I needed a power greater than myself. The AA group fit perfectly; I felt safe in the AA rooms. This conceptualization of a Higher Power began in a mechanistic manner that transformed into firm conviction. Ultimately, AA afforded gatherings of good people, and a welcoming place filled with the spirit of optimism where love and laughter prevail. *That* is *my* Higher Power.

Step Three - *Made a decision to turn our will and our lives over to the care of God, as we understood Him,* encourages trust in that power. (The independent thinker takes issue with the male pronoun and "being" associated with a higher power.) Nevertheless, armed with a desire for trust, we go to:

Step Four - *Made a searching and fearless moral inventory of ourselves,* which provides a basic introduction to an examined life.

Step Five - *Admitted to God, to ourselves, and to another human being, the exact nature of our wrongs,* involves a closer look at oneself and an acknowledgment of that perception to another person, not necessarily a belief in an invisible supernatural being. The practice of Step Five alleviates shame and promotes the ability to be OK with being oneself.

I'd always resolved to take my big secret, childhood sexual abuse, to the grave, which created unrelenting shame and guilt. After 15 years in AA, I was at a Fifth Step meeting with some AA brothers when I disclosed my dreadful secret. That experience paved the path to forgiveness of myself, not just for the shame and guilt related to the sexual abuse, but for my antisocial behavior driven by my substance abuse and lack of moral maturity. In the end, self-acceptance replaced self-loathing.

Step Six - *Were* entirely *ready to have God remove these defects of character.* On the surface, this step reflects the Calvinistic influences in AA, not only in its pathetically misleading language (*were entirely ready to have God remove these defects of character*), but in the narrow mindedness revealed in the opening text: *But when I ... asked God to give me release, my obsession to drink was vanished ... So, in a very complete and literal way, all AA's have become "entirely ready" to have God remove the mania for alcohol from their lives. And God has proceeded to do exactly that!* This ignores the rigorous spiritual journey that many AA's experience in communion with the collective, rendering the AA member a defective entity that must rely on the omnipotent power of God, an invisible male supernatural being.

However, the Step Six text ultimately contains a powerful message in self-awareness, taking one beyond "glaring and destructive" character flaws such as violence toward others, repeated lying, and stealing that bring consequences. It provides a means to focus on common character flaws that are often enjoyable and frequently overlooked. The result is a fine-tuning of awareness that leads to enlightenment and wisdom.

In mentoring young social workers, Step Six prompts me to question the desire I have to impress them with my wisdom, which, if overstated, can interfere with the basic premise of mentorship. Bill Wilson gently raises this point in Step Six with the questions, "*Who doesn't like to feel just a little superior to the next fellow?*" Other gems include: "*Do we sometimes let greed masquerade as ambition? ... Do we always try to help those we criticize or are we trying at times to proclaim our own righteousness and punish?*" For me, this basic design provided self-awareness, a path to self-forgiveness, and peace of mind. It's not a new idea. Several thousand years ago, Socrates proclaimed, "An unexamined life is a life that is not worth living."

Step Seven - *Humbly asked Him to remove our shortcomings.* Despite the vagueness and the magical-thinking simplicity of its title, the entire text of Step Seven explores humility from its origin in the Greek root—"to be human." I've concluded that this Step is a natural follow-up to a process that increases self-awareness in a group of folks not lacking in grandiosity.

Step Eight - *Made a list of all those we had harmed, and became willing to make amends to them all,* is a powerful reminder of membership in a universe of creation. In examining "the wreckage of the past," it provides a mechanism for the "fascinating adventure of learning how to live in peace, partnership, and brotherhood with all men and women."

Step Nine - *Made direct amends to such people wherever possible, except when to do so would injure them or others,* demonstrates a culminating progression. We addressed delusion in Step Two, where we examined repeated attempts to solve an ongoing problem utilizing a failed method and expecting different results—very primitive stuff. At Step Nine, we explore an executive ego function, decision-making: the ability to employ judgment in addressing life's entanglements.

Step Ten - *Continued to take personal inventory and when we were wrong promptly admitted it,* provides a system for awareness: A spot-check personal inventory during the day, a quick nightly inventory, and a periodic "housecleaning" with spiritual advisor(s). Step Ten sets the stage for immediate, daily, and ongoing practice. It also introduces the practice of responsibility, not just admitting "when we were wrong," but taking a stand "when we were right."

Step Eleven – *Sought through prayer and meditation to improve our conscious contact with God as we understood Him, praying only for the knowledge of His will for us and the power to carry that out,* opened the door to an inexhaustible exploration of spiritual search and study.

Step Twelve – *Having had a spiritual awakening as a result of these steps, we tried to carry this message to alcoholics and*

to practice these principles in all our affairs. This is a cove-
nant that can embrace not only alcoholics but the earth and
all its inhabitants.

Although a Twelve-Step partisan, I recognize that alternative methods of treatment for substance dependence have
merit and should not be discounted. Having said that, I am
convinced that alternatives or comparisons to Twelve-Step
practice are not evenly balanced. The principles associated
with Twelve-Step philosophies originated in Alcoholics Anonymous, where a meeting of two in 1935 grew to a community
of millions in many countries throughout the world. If you
include the well-documented impact on families of AA members, AA has arguably impacted favorably on the lives of tens
of millions of people throughout the world. This does not include the many companion societies of AA, such as Narcotics
Anonymous, Gamblers Anonymous, Debtors Anonymous, or
Overeaters Anonymous. By contrast, alternatives to AA such
as Smart Recovery, Rational Recovery, or Moderation Management are unable to establish ongoing meetings in any of
the outlying boroughs of New York City, despite years of concerted attempts. Comparing AA to these alternatives is like
comparing a Monet to a "paint by numbers." AA might not
be for everyone; not everyone who otherwise qualifies wants
AA. However, for those who are lost in substance dependence, there is no better way to find a reason for living and a
design for living.

8. HOME IN TENECK

In 1977, Ilene and I moved to Teaneck, a town that achieved national distinction in the early 1960s as the first municipality in the country to integrate its public schools voluntarily. Subsequently, the citizens of Teaneck welcomed an influx of new neighbors, who were schoolteachers, social workers, civil servants, and varied members of a diverse working and middle class. Teaneck became a diverse community and home to some famous people.

Theodora Lacey taught in the Teaneck school system for thirty-seven years. She and her husband, Dr. Archie Lacey, a prominent civil rights activist and educator, were close associates of Dr. Martin Luther King Jr., during the civil rights struggle in Birmingham and Selma. Theodora was also a close friend of Rosa Parks. The Lacey's arrived in Teaneck in the early 1960s, followed by many writers, artists, and famous athletes such as Howard Fast, Jim Bouton, Tony Campbell, Dave Winfield, Hilton Ruiz, Placido Domingo, Rufus Reed, Mike Kelly, Milt Jackson, Clyde McFadden and many others who found a home in Teaneck. Theodora taught both of my boys in middle school. Her husband, Archie, helped guide them through Sunday school in our Unitarian-Universalist church. Tony Campbell, of the New York Knicks, coached my son, Kevin, in all-star basketball.

At first, moving into a suburban home created anxiety for me. Having lived hand-to-mouth for much of my life, I dreaded the responsibilities of homeownership, but eventually, I caught on. Ilene and I spent the next thirty-six years turning our house into a family dwelling. Within the first few years of occupying the house, an AA brother, Irish Tommy, built an addition to accommodate our growing family. I had the opportunity to work with Tommy and his crew. I helped frame, did other rough carpentry, and built a deck. Ilene converted the yard into attractive flower, shrub, and vegetable gardens. As time passed, we grew more connected to our home.

The plan was for Ilene and me to start a family once we were married and became homeowners, but an infertility problem thwarted that plan for several years. After two years of unsuccessful infertility treatment, we decided on adoption. We started the process, which was fraught with disappointment and frustration for seven years, until the joyful arrival of twenty-three-day-old Kevin, who became our Hollywood epic. Two years later, we were blessed with another occasion of immense joy, the arrival of our second son, Brian. Participating in their journey to manhood while navigating life's rollercoaster was, at times, stressful, but overall, a wonderful experience that I never anticipated. My sons are a gift that keeps giving.

Shortly after Kevin's arrival, I re-established contact with my cousin, Dorothy, who lived in a neighboring town. I remember Dorothy as bright and gifted, always available to help navigate life's difficulties. Unfortunately, Uncle Joe believed that sending a girl to college was a waste of time and money. After high school, Dorothy went to work at Lamsten's Five & Ten while her two older brothers went on to prepare for careers in law and business. At an early age, Dorothy and I identified with each other as disposable people. Being eight years older than me in a large family, (she was eleven, and I was three when I arrived), she assumed much of the childcare activities. Dorothy told me that the arrival of a "new little brother" provided much joy in what otherwise was a rather somber life. She remembered a feeling of pride and wellbeing after helping me to dress up in freshly ironed clothes in preparation for our frequent walks on Church Avenue in Brooklyn.

We remained close until my departure eleven years later, when contact with her ended abruptly. However, she remained in my thoughts, and after reaching some stability in sobriety, I initiated contact, and we reconnected. After thirty years of mischief, which provided Dorothy with endless opportunities for prayer, the "prodigal boy" returned, complete with a Jewish wife and a black child. Despite growing up in a close "tribe," Dorothy recognized that we were living in a different world and welcomed her new African-American nephew with absolute delight.

By the time we reestablished contact, Dorothy's two children were out of the house and starting families of their own, so it was just her and her husband Walter in their spacious home in Dumont, New Jersey. I remember when Dorothy started to date Walter. She had a few previous boyfriends; I always felt indifferent toward them. But Walter stood apart. One night, I saw them kissing and heard Walter say, "I love you, Dottie." My immediate thought was, "This guy is going to take away my main ally." I was afraid of losing Dorothy, even though I knew she was unhappy at home. Gradually, I began to accept Walter as a good guy who could provide an escape for my "big sister."

Their wedding was somewhat of a milestone for me. At the age of twelve, I had my first alcohol blackout at the reception. I woke up the following morning with a tremendous hangover and full of fear, vowing to "never drink again." Years later, I would awaken almost daily, determined never to drink again, followed by the inevitable blackout when evening arrived. This pledge was repeated thousands of times before I got sober. Walter was an engineer. He had a fantastic job, which involved world travel to places in Europe, Africa, and South America. He loved his work and took Dorothy and the kids with him on his travels when school schedules permitted. At the age of sixty-three, Walter succumbed to a bone disease that resulted in a leg amputation. Since his job required hardhat participation at varying construction sites, he could no longer meet these demands and had to retire. Depression and anger replaced his humor and good fellowship. His drinking escalated as did his irrational anger: "Dorothy didn't put the mail in the right place;" noise from the vacuum disturbed his sense of peace; Dorothy was not appreciative of all the work he did to provide a home. His discontent with life was constant.

Walter had always liked his liquor, but could control it reasonably well. However, with his sense of importance greatly diminished by forced retirement, alcohol provided a balm for his despondency. As is the nature of the beast, alcohol quickly became the "rapacious creditor," requiring greater amounts with less enjoyment. By the time he reached sixty-four, Walter had become a full-blown alcoholic.

I attempted to convince Walter to get help, insisting that there was a better way to live, but he was not listening. Dorothy called me one morning, very upset because of Walter's morning whiskey drinking and increasing aggressiveness. When I asked if she was afraid for her safety, Dorothy said that she was not in the least bit worried about hand-to-hand conflict, stating that, if necessary, she could beat the crap out of him. What troubled her was his increasing unpredictable craziness, which proved to be a valid concern. Later that day, Walter got hold of the car keys, and in an attempt to stop him from driving, Dorothy stood in the driveway. She barely escaped injury as he attempted to run her down with the car, and in the process, crashed into the garage door. The police came and arrested Walter for drunk driving, and he stayed in the Bergen County Jail for two weeks. I visited Walter regularly as the severe culture shock of going to jail for the first time at sixty-four, where most of his fellow prisoners were young African-American men, overwhelmed him.

Walter pleaded, "Come on, Jimmy, you're a fuckin' social worker, get me out a' this dump." I reassured him, but also let him know that he needed help with his alcohol problem. This was indeed a role reversal. Dorothy provided respite for my darkened world in childhood. Now, as a sober social worker, I was able to help her.

Eventually, after some negotiation with the judicial system and potential treatment providers, Walter was accepted for treatment at a rehab in Connecticut. At the time, this was the only in-residence rehab in the tristate area that accepted Medicare for alcoholism treatment. I arranged for an AA brother, Andy, to transport Walter from the jail to the rehab. In addition to being an ex-drunk, Andy was a retired police officer who stood six feet seven. Walter, unfortunately, assumed that Andy was a chauffeur and ordered him to stop at a strip mall with a liquor store, so he could "pick up a few necessities." Andy stopped the car. He told Walter that it was a nice sunny day, that they could enjoy a pleasant trip, listening to music while witnessing the blossoming of spring. Or, if Walter insisted on challenging this plan, he could be handcuffed, and they would make the trip anyway. In agreeing to this violation of his civil liberties, Walter began his journey to sobriety, listening to music and observing pleasant scenery.

In 1985, I had the honor of presenting Walter with his ninety-day pin following his first three months of sobriety. Walter expressed gratitude at that celebration, remarking that although he still missed his work, he was embarking on a life of promise. He went on to develop a firm identification with AA, happy about having a sense of peace and wellbeing.

I was sitting with Walter before the start of our Tuesday night AA meeting when an old guy wandered into the room. On the verge of tears, he stated that he needed help because he couldn't stop drinking. Walter put a hand on his shoulder and guided him toward the kitchen. "You look like shit. Come with me; I'll buy you a cup of coffee." He went on to explain to the old guy that it's never too late to start living. Under Walter's guidance, the old guy got sober.

Walter went on to serve as a General Service Representative for that AA group in Teaneck. He served well and built a reputation for reliability and friendliness that outlived his passing in 1993, when he succumbed to brain cancer. Dorothy told me that in one of the last conversations she had with Walter in the hospital, he asked her, "Am I going to die?" She answered, "Yes, Walter." He smiled sheepishly and replied, "Well, you win some, and you lose some." His legacy lives on in the AA rooms.

Following Walter's passing, Dorothy sold the house in New Jersey and moved to a condo in Vero Beach, Florida, which was in a gated community with a private beach. Ilene, the kids, and I visited her during the winter of 1994. With the possible exception of domestic servants and groundskeepers, Kevin and Brian were the only black faces in the whole place. Upon waking up the first morning, the boys raced toward the beach. A security officer saw them and followed in hot pursuit, yelling that it was a private beach, and they were not allowed on it. Dorothy glanced out the window, saw what was happening, and joined the fracas, shouting at the security officer that these kids were her nephews and had every right to be on the beach. The episode culminated in all parties colliding together, out of breath, with the security officer profusely apologizing to Dorothy and the boys. Dorothy graciously accepted the apology, and the boys were left smiling in anticipation of their swim.

Dorothy is gone now. I never spoke to her about the sexual abuse I had encountered in her childhood home. I'm fairly certain that she was a victim herself, and the subject was just too painful. She is gone, but her loving kindness remains an important memory etched in the recesses of my being.

While I lived in Teaneck, I commuted daily to my job in the South Bronx, a short trip but worlds apart from Teaneck. On many occasions, I brought Kevin and Brian with me.

Both have fond memories of the South Bronx, where they met special people. Kevin, then five, had a friend his age, Danny, who lived in a homeless shelter with his parents. When Kevin asked why Danny and his mom and dad didn't have a house, I told him that they were poor; they didn't have the money to get a house. Kevin questioned why they didn't just go to the bank like Mom does and get money, which led to a few discussions on the subject of poverty. While beginning to understand the basics of the topic, Kevin suggested that Danny and his parents could move into our house. He could share Brian's room with Brian, and his room could squeeze in three people. Explaining why this wouldn't work was somehow more difficult than talking about other matters. It reminds me of the story of my childhood friend getting slapped for his question, "Where do babies come from?" I've come to realize that although sex can be a challenging topic, it's more difficult to explain poverty to children than to talk to them about sex. How do you explain to a kid that we live on a planet that produces more than enough material goods to house and feed everyone, yet many of the planet's inhabitants are without homes and adequate food? To a rational budding mind, this is absurd. I wanted Kevin to understand that we live in an imperfect world, and it's our job to try to make it a better place.

Perhaps the most remarkable person the boys met in the South Bronx was Chief, an African who came to the United States as a young child. Chief was a street merchant. He had a table on 149th Street, where he sold African artifacts and provided community residents with ongoing discussions on current topics that were laced with humor and optimism. So, in addition to being a street merchant, he was also a street philosopher, considered by many to be a man of wisdom. Chief spoke several African languages, in addition to being fluent in Spanish and English. Both of my boys were quite impressed with Chief, who introduced them to African culture and provided them with leather pouches, where to this day, they keep treasures. Chief returned to Africa in the mid-1990s. Although we lost contact, his memory remains.

A few years later, I was driving Brian and his friend, Tommy, a bi-racial boy, to basketball practice when I overheard Brian describing Chief. "He's smart, he speaks many languages, he's not light-skinned like us, he's very black, a real African. He gave me this crystal that I wear around my neck; it has magic. You know what he told me? He said I am a 'righteous little brother.'" Tommy said, "Wow!"

Brian knew everyone. We were in the supermarket when he was six, and two moms and their kids, who I didn't know, greeted him heartily, on two separate occasions. "There's Brian. Hi, Brian."I thought, "How does a kid with limited unsupervised opportunities get to know so many people?" From an early age, Brian projected a zest for life.

His friend, Malcolm, was a nerd, an African-American nerd—short, chubby, bespectacled, athletically-challenged, and not interested in hip hop. Some of his more enlightened contemporaries took pleasure in demeaning and ridiculing him, until Brian, with his innate sense of justice and disdain for bullying, established himself as Malcolm's protector. Brian and Malcolm became friends. Malcolm delighted in watching his friend's exploits on the basketball court and the football field, while Brian was introduced to Malcolm's free-spirited interest in the natural world.

One evening, Malcolm decided to take a shortcut home and attempted to cross Route 4 during the twilight hours. He was struck by an SUV and died a few hours later. Brian, consumed with grief and anger, was inconsolable. Attempts to comfort him were met with sobbing rage. Aware of Malcolm's obliviousness to danger and the need for protection, Brian could not reconcile this tragic loss. He did not attend Malcolm's memorial service; in fact, it would take several years before he could attend any memorial service. However, Brian wrote a moving eulogy that was printed in Teaneck High's yearbook. Brian now lives in Texas and works in a residential facility for troubled boys. "Malcolm—R.I.P." is tattooed on his left arm.

As Kevin got older, he developed a clearer understanding of his world. When he was nine, Kevin showed an interest in cooking, which was inspired by the many gatherings at the Smith home. Jannie and Willie Smith arrived in Teaneck from the rural South, bringing Teaneck their deep-rooted Southern African-American cultural experiences. The Smith family grew to include two boys, Sheldon and Jonah, who became classmates and eventually, best friends (and adopted cousins) of Kevin and Brian's.

During the many family gatherings and sleepovers at the Smith's, Kevin received rudimentary cooking instructions from "Auntie Jannie"—ham hocks and collard greens, cornbread, barbeque, southern fried chicken, and other culinary treasures. He also baked with me at home, producing his first unassisted sweet potato pie at the age of ten. Our Unitarian-Universalist congregation provided an opportunity for volunteer work at soup kitchens and homeless shelters, which paved the way for his promotion to the status of culinary craftsman. Kevin, now in his early thirties, is the Executive Chef at the famed Cloverleaf Tavern in Caldwell, New Jersey. He still volunteers at soup kitchens and shelters in Newark and Paterson.

About ten years ago, Kevin came home with a tattoo artist friend who proceeded to add to the abundance of ink on Kevin's arms. Ilene and I were in the kitchen, and she exclaimed, "I'd like to get a tattoo. I think I'll see if Kevin's friend can do a butterfly. What do you think?" I said I thought it was a good idea as long as she avoided her neck and face. She laughed, remarking that she planned to use discretion and went upstairs to Kevin's room. Five minutes later, Brian appeared in a state of distress. "Mom's getting tattooed, you've got to stop her. Mothers aren't supposed to get tattoos." I explained that when I was his age, women wore earrings and men got tattoos, but now things are different. Since Brian had been wearing an earring since he was twelve years old, this gave him food for thought. Subsequently, Ilene, the sixty-year-old Renaissance woman, displayed a beautiful butterfly just below her left shoulder.

With the gradual corporatization of the healthcare system, it is no longer possible to bring children to most workplaces. When a clerical worker at Fordham-Tremont, a single-parent mom, brought her young daughter to work because the child-care center was closed, St. Barnabas administration informed her they did not allow children in the workplace. She had to sacrifice an entitled day off, such as vacation or personal day, and take her daughter home.

It was fortunate that both of my boys had the opportunity to visit the South Bronx on many occasions. They had the opportunity for friendships with folks like Danny and the Chief, in addition to meeting and getting to know a variety of my co-workers, clients, and community residents. When I contemplate the contrast to my growing up, I experience a feeling of gratitude—life started pretty poorly for me, but with Mom never giving up on me and the love and guidance of mentors, life has since been good, and my boys have benefited. Unfortunately, these simple opportunities no longer exist in today's world, a world with advanced technology concurrent with decreasing interpersonal connection. Bring children to work? The current powers-that-be declare that it would impede production and reduce profit.

In 1977, Ilene and I began graduate school in social work, with Ilene at NYU and me at Columbia. The Columbia School of Social Work provided a rare and enlightening experience because of the collective wisdom of a group of exceptional mentors: Hy Weiner, Irving Miller, Mary Goldson, and Alex Gitterman. These folks were not just academics, but true progressives. I wish I had the opportunity to revisit my time at Columbia. One of the consequences of growing up late in life is I missed many of the finer points of social work education. My lack of maturity manifested in political absolutism and arrogance. Ideas that I disagreed with, I simply dismissed as irrelevant and didn't investigate the possibility of whether or not they had merit.

I remember when Al Gitterman had to restore order in class after I got into it with another student I perceived as being anti-union. Although I realized that I hadn't handled the situation well, I believed that I was right, and my adversary was absolutely wrong. It wasn't until several years later that I could acknowledge the truth expressed by adversaries. I believe that this lesson began in AA: Be quick to listen and slow to condemn. Listen! Learn to listen and then listen to learn.

This lesson began to seriously take root following an incident that demanded self-examination. Several of my Freedom and Peace friends and I (two guys and three gals) rode in a convertible with the top down on Route 4 in New Jersey. A U.S. Army truck with a bunch of soldiers occupied the adjoining lane. The soldiers waved to the girls, and the girls waved back, all smiles. I shouted at the top of my lungs, "Get the fuck out of Vietnam!" All merriment abruptly ceased, smiles disappeared, and one young soldier looked as if he were about to cry. One of my companions said, "Why did you say that?" I responded that these guys were taking part in a racist, genocidal attack on the people of Vietnam—as if that made my outburst rational. I knew what I did was wrong and felt embarrassed, but I couldn't admit it at the time. Self-examination was in order.

AA's Fourth Step (*Made a searching and fearless moral inventory of ourselves*), provided guidance. In all probability, the young men on the back of that truck got drafted. They neither started the fight in Vietnam nor personally elected to go there and kill its citizens. They might have believed that they were serving their country, a noble enterprise. But in keeping with the axiom that sustains ignorance—"contempt prior to investigation"—I judged with certitude and played the fool. This is an example of growing up late in life; it's hard.

Despite years of despair, a spark of hope, however tiny, was planted by Aunt Mary, Ham, the Irish nun, Father Tom, Joe Flaherty, and others from my working-class community. This spark helped me survive until other good people arrived and invited me into their gatherings where the spark strengthened. After completing social work school, I left the city methadone program and went to work at the Albert Einstein College of Medicine, Division of Substance Abuse. I supervised addiction counselors in the methadone program there, a job that introduced a social work experience in the South Bronx that spanned thirty-six years. I worked in the Hub area on 149th Street near 3rd Avenue, the virtual Main Street of the South Bronx. Gerena Valentin, a city council member at that time, had an office across the street from where I worked. Our association blossomed into a memorable learning experience.

Gerena migrated from Lares, Puerto Rico to New York City in 1937, a year after I was born. After coming to the mainland, he worked as a hotel dishwasher and, after serving in the U.S. Army during World War II, returned and began a lifetime commitment to progressive political activities. Starting as a union organizer for Puerto Rican hotel workers, he went on to work in community organization and leadership, emphasizing the need for working-class unity in the struggle against class injustice and racism. Throughout the 1950s, Gerena was closely associated with Vito Marcantonio, a leading congressional progressive and founder of the American Labor Party. In 1963, he shared the podium with Dr. Martin Luther King

Jr. in Washington, D.C., when King delivered his famous "I Have a Dream" speech. In addition to his leading role in the founding of the Puerto Rican Day Parade and other cultural activities in New York City, he served as a city councilman from 1977 to 1981. In 1982, Gerena helped develop and became the first chairman of the New Alliance Party. In 1985, Gerena returned to Lares, Puerto Rico, where he remained politically active until his passing at the age of 98.

I had the opportunity to work on a reelection campaign for Gerena, which led to several meaningful conversations with this great man. One of the subjects of these conversations was my serious reservations about methadone treatment that I continue to have. Gerena advised that I remain employed in methadone treatment, implying that methadone is here to stay and is so powerful that efforts to correct it not only have a good chance of failing but would possibly siphon energies from more immediate issues. Since it is here to stay, and it does prevent some from going to jail, it is essential that progressives are involved. So, I elected to remain in the South Bronx methadone clinic. This decision turned out to be a good one.

Unfortunately, between 1977 and 1980, I still had more drinking to do. During this time, I went out on three, one-day drinking binges that were followed by Ilene taking me "by the ear" back to AA. My drinking career ended with a whimper rather than a crescendo. My last drink, a half-bottle of white wine, took place on October 13, 1980. The very next day, my sponsor, Bill McGovern, took me on a Twelve-Step call. It is generally considered bad practice for an alcoholic who is counting his sobriety in hours to attempt Twelve-Step work, but Bill believed that this situation called for an exception. At the request of a young woman, we went to Jersey City to visit her dad, who we found passed out on a couch lying in his own filth. We got him cleaned up and took him to a detox facility where he was admitted. This was not a regular Twelve-Step call in that the old man was in no shape to listen to an AA message. He desperately needed medical treatment, but this was before the advent of 911 calls. Bill said to me, "I'm glad that you had an opportunity to see your future self." I suddenly remembered the nurse from many years ago, whose metaphorical perception of Coney Island Max with drool on his chin was now reflected in this old man's condition. I thought, "Holy shit, that's me!" This was indeed a moment of clarity. I have not had a drink since.

9. RACISM IS INSIDIOUS

Shortly after our move to Teaneck, Ilene and I became involved in Teaneck politics. We recognized that the school board and the Town Council were pivotal institutions that required a lot of energy to maintain the high standards of Teaneck's mission. Together with a formidable group of progressives, we attended Town Council meetings and Board of Ed meetings. We served on committees and helped elect progressive candidates. We believed in our town and rejoiced in its diversity. Then came the Philip Pannell incident.

On an April night in 1990, a 16-year-old African-American boy was shot to death by a white police officer in Teaneck. The boy, Philip Pannell, was running away from the officer. The officer, Gary Spath, shot him in the back. According to Spath, Pannell was reaching for a gun in his jacket pocket, and Spath believed that his life was in danger. Witnesses, however, claimed that Pannell's arms were raised in surrender. Although he had never killed a suspect, Spath had a well-documented history of inappropriately drawing and firing his weapon. This situation provided fertile ground for polarization. Civil rights leaders and community activists from near and far, drawing on the history of police brutality in African-American communities, took notice. So did law-and-order proponents who believed that police officers were disrespected and often in danger when policing African-American communities.

At the time, I was serving on a Town Council advisory committee on substance abuse that included members of the clergy, law enforcement, and social services. We had a meeting scheduled for April 10, 1990, the day of the incident. As chairman, I started to phone the eight committee members to remind them of the meeting. The first call was to Bob Adomelli, a Teaneck police officer who told me that he would not attend the meeting because an officer had shot a black kid on the northeast side. He seemed quite distraught and abruptly hung up. That was my introduction to the Pannell incident, followed by town meetings, vigils, protests, and youth riots, which gained national attention in the coming months.

Bob Adomelli, a good guy who exemplified nobility in his ongoing efforts to protect the community, was a friend of Gary Spath. I didn't like the idea of being on opposing sides with him on this very troubling issue. However, Bob's involvement in the Pannell incident proved to be a learning experience for me.

Brian Burke, Teaneck's police chief, issued a gag order. Members of the police department were forbidden to attend any meetings or discussions related to the Pannell incident. Adomelli believed the order was a grave error that would contribute to the town's polarization. He, therefore, ignored the directive and attended several meetings, never wavering in his support for his friend, Gary Spath, while listening to and acknowledging the opinions of all.

I brought four-year-old Brian to a Pannell vigil outside of the Teaneck townhouse. Adomelli was on duty that day. Although not in uniform, he wore his badge on a chain around his neck. He noticed me and came over to say hello. I introduced him to Brian, who asked him if he was a policeman. When Bob responded that he was, Brian asked, "Where's your gun?" Bob laughed as he explained that it wasn't always necessary to display a gun, particularly at a prayer vigil. When he was leaving, Bob affectionately patted Brian on the back and told him that he had a good dad. Sometime later, Bob remarked to me that I was the "real deal," a real liberal—as opposed to the white liberals who love black people as long as they don't move next door to them. Although not completely agreeing with his perception, I was quite pleased with the compliment and thanked Bob.

In local committee work, I also got to know Jack Terhune, Dean Kazinci, Dave Kelter, and Gary Fiedler, all prominent representatives of the Teaneck Police Department. Jack Terhune and I had meaningful contact because we were involved in our sons' Little League. In the mid-1980s, Jack was elected Bergen County Sheriff on the Republican ticket. When I informed him that he was the first Republican I had voted for since John Lindsey, he replied that he was not particularly interested in party politics. The only reason he ran on a Republican ticket was because Republicans offered him the opportunity and he wanted the job.

As sheriff, Terhune assumed directorship of the Bergen County Jail. Within our many conversations, he told me that the only difficulty he had with AA and NA meetings at the jail was that there wasn't enough space to accommodate all the meetings. Jack believed that drug treatment is a necessary alternative to incarceration for addicts and alcoholics. The drug program that he started at the Bergen County Jail has evolved into a model reentry program that has since expanded. Terhune was, perhaps, the first local law enforcement official to address mass incarceration. However, I was in complete disagreement with his vigorous support of Spath, which I believe contributed to the repeated occurrences of white police officers killing black citizens and getting away with it.

Nevertheless, I discovered that Spath was not a conscious racist, more likely a racist who didn't know he was a racist. I learned that Freddy Greene, the well-respected first African-American to join the Teaneck Police Department, was an early mentor and friend of Spath. Luis Torres, who joined Greene as one of the four non-white officers in the Teaneck Police Department, went on to develop an abiding friendship with Spath. The Torres and Spath families often socialized together; the men had common interests in sports, went fishing, and helped each other in the maintenance of their respective homes. Torres reported that he had never been invited to the homes of any of his white fellow officers before Gary Spath had joined the department.

After much soul-searching, Torres concluded that Pannell's death was related to his friend's impulsivity and was totally unnecessary. Although other officers had the same opinion but did not express it, Torres' openly expressed opinion resulted in ostracism by his colleagues. Thus, an example of how "the blue wall of silence" calcifies polarization.

A glaring illustration of this silent blue wall occurred in 1992 when after his acquittal, the Detective Crime Bureau, a prominent law enforcement organization, awarded Spath "Policeman of the Month." The decision to give Spath this award was far from unanimous. However, those who were opposed abstained rather than vote no. During the awards ceremony, the Nutley Police Department was given an award for its innovation in community policing. In accepting the award, the mayor of Nutley acknowledged Spath, stating, "What happened to you shouldn't have happened to a dog. I have no sympathy for criminals. I'm very proud when you blow them away." The fact that this guy was not booed off the podium is indicative of many police departments' unwillingness to challenge wrongdoing in their ranks.

I was asked by representatives of the progressive community to prepare a presentation on the Pannell incident and deliver it to the Town Council. The meeting was moved from the Council chambers to a school auditorium to accommodate a potentially large crowd. I declined. I was not comfortable speaking to such a large audience. Or so I said. The truth is, despite my fury over this issue, I feared confronting police officers that I ultimately respected. It was a time when the population was so acutely polarized that there wasn't much room for nuance.

Progressives were inclined to believe that all white cops were racist. In contrast, many supporters of the police thought that police officers could do no wrong in attempting to provide order to groups of the morally challenged. I knew that this was not true, but I was in the process of evolving from self-loathing to self-awareness, and I struggled with self-doubt. I didn't yet fully realize that I had valid opinions that counted for something. In looking back at this gradual change in my thinking, I am grateful for all my mentors—from the Irish nun and Ham Allen to the sisters and brothers in AA, to the many friends whose understanding and love have helped heal my wounds. Right now, in the 21st century, I'm okay being "me" but if I had the opportunity to do it over, I would address that Town Council with honesty and conviction.

I would tell them of my experiences in a white working-class community, a community where a significant proportion of the young men became police officers (that is those who managed to stay out of the youth house and juvenile detention). I would tell them how many of these young men were assigned to communities of color in an attempt to mitigate centuries of structural racism. I would tell them that most of these young men fell into the systemic undoing of law enforcement principles, where, instead of protecting communities, they exercised custodial control, backed by violence—and then some bragged about it. I would tell them I witnessed friends who became police officers increasingly spouting racial slurs and only trusting fellow police officers. I would also tell them of a small minority of police officers who disavowed racism and viewed their job as protectors and peacekeepers. I would tell them that this tragedy presents an opportunity for honest discussion combined with mutual respect.

But, of course, I couldn't say that to a 1990s Town Council. I can't undo what was done. I can, however, forgive myself for cowardice and use it as a learning experience. I remember doing an AA Fourth Step (*Made a searching and fearless moral inventory of ourselves)* and recalling past shameful behavior where I thought, "I hope God forgives me because I don't forgive me." I realize now that self-forgiveness can come *with* self-examination. As author, Ariel Leve, eloquently noted in a *New York Times* book review: "Refugees from a turbulent childhood are never truly at home in adulthood." That has been an ongoing challenge in my struggle to transform self-loathing into self-respect.

The Philip Pannell story provides an essential lesson in the matter of race relations. Before the incident, I was comfortable believing that Teaneck was a model town that valued equality, without giving much thought to the historical complexities of racism. However, I came to understand that although Teaneck was a diverse community, it was mostly segregated. The northeast section was predominately black, and the northwest section was predominately white, while the remainder was somewhat mixed. Overall, there was limited social interaction between the races. Teaneck High School was about fifty-percent black, and there was an unofficial "black door" and "white door" at the high school. The police department was approximately ninety-five percent white. Black kids, for the most part, did not trust white police officers and black people and white people did not normally engage in mutual family and social activity.

In contemplating my identity as a white person, I think of Andrew Hacker's monumental work, *Two Nations, Black and White—Separate, Hostile, and Unequal,* where he speaks of the symbolism of looking in a mirror and seeing a white face, the norm. I can identify with white being the norm. Schools taught and pulpits preached that whiteness is the norm, and non-whiteness is "the other." Irrespective of *my* self-appraisal and *my* self-worth, the "other" was a fact of life reinforced by family and community. I believe that identifying darker-skinned people as "the other" is the bedrock of structural racism, no matter how liberal you are. When Gary Spath aimed his weapon at Philip Pannell, he was confronting "the other," invoking centuries of white fear and mistrust, one of the reasons why black kids don't trust white police officers, and why social interaction between the races is limited. Among the complexities of structural racism in America, "the other" stands out as a major component.

Complicating Philip Pannell's status as "the other" was the fact that he was a gang member, and he carried a starter pistol redesigned into a weapon that could fire .22 caliber bullets. Reliable reports stated that he was in fear for his life and carried the weapon as a means of protection. Because of his father's drinking problem and the accompanying family instability, the Pannell family had difficulty in establishing a permanent address, although its roots were in Teaneck. When the Pannell's moved to the neighboring town of Englewood, Philip was mandated to attend school there. That was a problem for Philip. Englewood was home to a rival gang; consequently, he was in constant fear of attack, and thus the gun. Yet, based on several anecdotal reports from adults and peers who knew him, Philip Pannell was a friendly kid, fun-loving, although at times impulsive, and at times immature—a description befitting most teenage boys. Nobody described him as being potentially dangerous.

There is evidence that Gary Spath, like Philip Pannell, was a troubled teen, having had difficulties in at least two high schools. Mike Kelly, author and columnist for *The Record*, explored the Pannell incident in a 532-page book that turned out to be a masterful piece of journalism—*Color Lines: The Troubled Dreams of Racial Harmony in an American Town*. Kelly describes Spath as friendly, tolerant, and courageous while documenting a history of the inappropriate use of his weapon. When fellow officers Freddy Greene and Luis Torres questioned their friend about an appearance of impulsivity in the use of his gun in prior instances, Spath became defensive and dismissive, seeming to imply fear of "the other." The question becomes: Can one oppose race hatred and, at the same time, view people of color as "the other?"

My personal experience reveals that racism is a deeply ingrained contaminate in the soul of America. I was never a hardcore racist; I fit somewhere within the category of a racist who doesn't know he's a racist, my indifference to Jim Crow in Florida as a glaring example. From the time I acquired language, I was subtly (and not so subtly) taught that poverty among African Americans is the result of an inability to succeed. However, Ham, the Irish nun, and jazz provided counterbalancing experiences. But the predominant lesson I received as a child was that people with darker skin than me are "the other." It wasn't until I experienced the "other" in personal relationships that my perception began to change.

In Chicago, on the way to Cook County Jail in a paddy wagon, I witnessed a police officer beat a handcuffed black prisoner who was sitting next to me. Because we came from the white North Side, all of the prisoners were white except this one guy. He said nothing, nor did he do anything to warrant this attack. The officer made it clear that the reason for the attack was that he was a "nigger." Despite my general indifference, I was concerned for him, as blood flowed from his nose and he was visibly scared. But I did nothing. In my terror, I even felt grateful for white privilege. Half a century later, it still resonates with alarm. That incident compellingly challenged the myth that black people are perpetrators of violence against whites.

In 1951, a petition was presented to the United Nations, charging the United States with genocide. It documented over one-thousand specific incidents of violence and death that targeted African Americans during a four-year period. These crimes took place not only in the South but in almost every geographic area of the United States. The perpetrators included police, white nationalist mobs, institutions, and random individuals fueled by racism. Evidently, this documentation is incomplete because the Civil Rights Congress of 1950 reported that, "The murder of Negroes is so common as to render it impossible to keep an accurate account..."

One account randomly selected from the petition stated: *On August 15, 1945, sixteen-year-old Lila Bella Carter of Pine Island, South Carolina, was raped and murdered by a white man. Her neck and jaw were broken. When her father went to the authorities to demand an investigation, he was jailed. No action was taken against the rapist.*

Unfortunately, this story of Ms. Carter, as well as the entire 1951 petition, was mainly ignored by the media. The only acknowledgment made by most news outlets was a cold-war-related response linking the principal authors, William Patterson and Paul Robeson, to a Soviet-backed Communist conspiracy. Ultimately, the UN did not acknowledge receiving the petition, and attacks on African Americans continued.

When Bill O'Reilly was on *Fox News*, he stated that Black Lives Matter should be designated as a hate group, bent on violence toward white people. That is a continuation of a theme repeated throughout history from the black codes of the post-reconstruction period, instituted to protect white people from the so-called violence and sexual depravity of blacks, followed by Richard Nixon and Ronald Reagan's perpetration of white fear, to Donald Trump's embrace of white nationalism by identifying people of color as rapists, criminals, and terrorists.

My personal experience gives credence to this blatant distortion. I am a product of open enrollment. Without open enrollment, I would have had to make up three years of high school work prior to taking college courses, for which I had neither the energy nor the time. African-American activists opened the door of the City University, and I walked through. Opposition to open enrollment came from liberals as well as conservatives who believed that open enrollment would result in the deterioration of New York City's higher education. They pictured unmotivated, unprepared students invading city universities and crippling advanced learning. A respected, white community activist from Teaneck remarked that City University used to enable children of immigrants to acquire the finest education available. She proclaimed the advent of open enrollment was the destruction of higher education for the working class in New York City. That is entirely at odds with my experience.

I do not believe that this Teaneck activist was acquainted with the real outcome of open enrollment. Shirley Rodriguez, the director of a treatment program that provides service to a client population of 1,500 residents in the South Bronx, is a respected and proficient leader whose administrative competence is exceeded only by her superior clinical skills. Shirley is a product of open enrollment. Dr. Jose Torres, a respected medical director at the Albert Einstein College of Medicine, distinguished himself as an innovator in the treatment of HIV infestation and substance abuse. Jose is a product of open enrollment. Shirley and Jose, in addition to many of my colleagues at AECOM and Fordham-Tremont, are just part of countless success stories that began with open enrollment. I am proud to be a part of this group.

"Stop and frisk," a police practice that ostensibly targeted young men of color for suspicion of criminal activity, was ultimately deemed unconstitutional and racist, with no evidence of having reduced crime. My son, Kevin, was on his way to Port Authority, returning home from his job. Two police officers stopped him and proceeded to spill out the contents of his backpack. When he asked the officers why he was being stopped, they told him to "shut up." After finding no drugs or weapons, the officers left the scene with no apology, leaving the contents of Kevin's backpack on the sidewalk and Kevin devastated.

On the surface, it looks like the purveyors of oppression are winning in light of Trump's ascendance and his minions of haters. But there is a growing number of Americans who challenge injustice, and while the shrinking number of haters gets louder, bolder, and more desperate, there is precedent for optimism. I saw this play out in my union when the criminals who took control decreased in numbers but increased in intensity only to be drowned out by an enlightened membership a little over thirty years ago.

Even small doses of optimism can be remarkable. A situation involving a middle-aged woman who was an outpatient at Fordham-Tremont comes to mind. She was exhibiting a severe psychotic break in the waiting room, and presented a threat to the safety of all, including herself. A 911 call alerted emergency medical services, followed by the arrival of a team of three police officers. During moments of clarity in this woman's life, I knew her as a frightened person who often struggled with conflicting messages of internal terrors juxtaposed with external reality. When this episode began, her inner terror was winning. The thought saddened me that she would probably be restrained (handcuffed) and forcibly taken to the hospital. "I ain't goin' to no fuckin' hospital!" However, the officers restored calm. The team leader spoke to her softly in Spanish, convincing her that she was going to a safe place while the other two officers exuded a sense of protection. She was then transported to the hospital, unrestrained. I had to ask myself, "Are these the same guys who do stop and frisk?"

That was not an isolated incident; I have witnessed many similar events. Like the spirit of optimism found in AA meetings and in the words of great American thinkers such as Barack Obama and Pete Seeger, optimism can be a forceful state of mind. Nineteenth-century explorer, Ernest Shackleton, perhaps said it best: "Optimism is moral courage."

Historically, police departments were co-opted as a government-backed apparatus that served the interests of the rich. They were used to disrupt civil rights protests and to act as strikebreakers, and to be active agents of "stop and frisk" assaults. Although there are police officers who are motivated by racism and a need to control, one cannot overlook the systemic influences that produce a "stop and frisk" mentality among police officers who simply wish to serve. Perhaps a step in counterbalancing this problem is by merging social work values and law enforcement principles. These two noble professions could learn from each other.

Many police officers, because of the stressful and dangerous nature of their jobs, opt for "twenty and out," retirement after twenty years of service. These relatively young retirees are prime candidates for the profession of social work. The National Association of Social Workers and social work schools would benefit from reaching out to them. Their invaluable experiences would undoubtedly enrich the social work profession. A police officer, retired at 40, can transition into social work via graduate school and social work practice until 60, and continue a career as a faculty member in a social work graduate school where she would bring the richness of a lifetime experience in addressing social conflict.

In retirement from police work, Gary Spath has expressed a desire to enter the counseling profession. I wish him well and hope that his experience with Philip Pannell will provide him with a foundation for spiritual examination and growth that leads to an ability to help others.

10. 1199, MY UNION

The Teaneck move coincided with the gratifying beginnings of my 28-year affiliation with Local 1199/SEIU, a union that Martin Luther King Jr. called his favorite union. The AECOM 1199 chapter, led by Bernie Minter, was one of the most active and militant chapters that this union ever produced. I had the good fortune to work with and learn from many outstanding people that include leaders such as Bernie, Angela Doyle, Joe James, Dennis Rivera, Eddie Kay, and Marshall Garcia, in addition to a host of rank and file activists.

Union work was challenging and rewarding. Although I had previous experience with trade unionism in the tent company, the water company, and the Boston bartenders union, 1199 was a brand-new experience. Most trade unions strive for democracy where every member has a voice, and 1199 is eminently successful at promoting democracy. The union president has power but can be overruled by the executive committee. The executive committee has power but can be overruled by the delegate assembly. The delegate assembly has power but can be overruled by the membership. This is what's known as "trickle-up."

Although still learning in 1979, I was able to contribute because of my personal experience. As a delegate, I realized that a significant percentage of union grievances were related to personal problems such as alcoholism, other substance abuse, or emotional stress. That was during a time when employee assistance programs, or "EAPs," were just gaining prominence. The premise of EAPs was that if a worker has a problem that is affecting their job performance, addressing the issue and returning the worker to a more productive status rather than firing the problem worker would be more cost effective than hiring and training a new worker.

When I suggested that we consider a union-based EAP program, the immediate response was negative. "Why would we tell the boss that our people have issues? That's only going to cause problems" was a typical response. Bernie Minter was among the most vociferous skeptics, but as a student of the dialectical form of fair-and-balanced analysis, he investigated before arriving at a conclusion. He read literature on EAPs and spoke to Dr. Lala Straussner of NYU. Lala is an authority on substance abuse treatment and employee assistance programs.

Bernie, a tough labor leader who instilled fear in bosses, and Lala, a college professor, and prominent author, may have had different temperaments and associations, but both had strong roots in the Jewish community. Their long conversation, including shared "Yiddishisms," left Bernie with a conviction that an EAP could have significant value to workers at AECOM. Thus, Bernie moved from skeptic to advocate. Incidentally, Lala Straussner made it possible for me to serve on a National Association of Social Workers chapter committee on alcoholism in the mid-1970s, which she chaired and then became my principal advisor and mentor in the NYU doctoral program. Lala's a significant person in my life.

Eventually, under the guidance of Bernie, the chapter leadership became firmly convinced that an EAP would provide needed services to many of our members, and in the process, would enhance job security. Following serious negotiation with management, an AECOM employee-assistance program was established. I had the honor of serving as coordinator for the next two years. As the EAP coordinator, I was relieved of many direct responsibilities and called to address job-related problems within the chapter. The vast majority of interventions involved substance abuse, primarily alcohol.

EAP work was a tremendous learning experience, not only in union matters but also in the practice of social work. I remember leaving an administrative hearing with a substantial amount of egg on my face after attempting to defend a member on principle, without investigating the facts. The member presented a history of alcohol abuse and a desperate need to get help. He neglected to inform me of two previous alcohol-related incidents when he signed out of detox against medical advice and resumed drinking immediately. He also neglected to disclose his history of repeated altercations with supervisors and coworkers. Unfortunately, I chose to defend this guy based on his best intentions without researching his actual behavior. That was a critical lesson, reminding me to think and investigate before yelling.

Perhaps what prompted this zealotry was that in 1955, the American Medical Association recognized alcoholism as an illness. I wanted to convince the world that this was true, that alcoholics aren't bad people, and substance dependence is an illness that is often life-threatening. But I didn't help this member. In fact, I inadvertently contributed to his problem. Given a do-over, I would have established clarity about the reality of his life rather than come to his rescue. I don't know what became of this person. He got fired and left, consumed with resentment. I hope that he eventually discovered that treatment works and that there is a better way to live.

Fortunately, most EAP interventions ended on a more positive note. "Cathy" was an administrative clerk and member of our bargaining unit. She appeared a little confused and slightly agitated upon entering my office, her breath broadcasting the distinct odor of alcohol. Cathy explained that her boss was exaggerating minor difficulties that put her job at risk. Since she was a single parent with two young children, losing her job would be disastrous. When I inquired if drinking had anything to do with the situation, she claimed that she drinks occasionally but is in complete control, stating that she hadn't had a drink for almost a week. I asked how alcohol had gotten on her breath. She said that she drank a "Mosey" (non-alcoholic beer) before our meeting. Cathy was in serious denial. I gently advised her that if she wished to save her job, she had to appear in my office the next morning at 9 am and not drink before the appointment. I showed her a breathalyzer and said that the presence or absence of alcohol in her system would be scientifically determined. Following an illogical rant of resistance, she agreed to the plan.

The next morning, Cathy arrived punctually, a little disheveled and shaky. Her breathalyzer results revealed a trace of alcohol, probably the residue of the previous night's debauch, but she was not under the influence. We explored Cathy's drinking history, attempts to stop, and concluded that she needed treatment. She agreed. What we didn't agree on was the method. I strongly suggested residential care while she was adamantly opposed to being "locked up." "Who will take care of my children while I'm away?" was her legitimate concern.

Often, single-parent women who face hospitalization for any reason are put in a "Sophie's Choice" situation. If Cathy continued to drink, her children would conceivably suffer irreparable harm. If placed in the foster care system while she was in treatment, there was potential for harm to her children. I do not doubt that the United States, the wealthiest country in the world, could easily incorporate family integrity into its healthcare system, but we have yet to arrive at that point in our evolution.

Fortunately, Cathy's mom and sister were able to help. We scheduled a family meeting that involved a discussion of repeated disappointments, enabling gestures, and eventual disengagement, typical of family alcoholism. Once they turned their attention to successful treatment outcomes, Cathy's mom and sister embraced a plan. Her sister agreed to care for the children while Cathy was away at treatment, and both sister and mom offered to attend family meetings at the rehab facility that Cathy chose. In those days, before managed care, 1199 had access to some of the best alcohol treatment facilities available.

Cathy got sober! A few years later, I had the opportunity to witness the celebration of her third anniversary in AA. After identifying herself as an alcoholic, Cathy expressed gratitude to God, to Alcoholics Anonymous, and 1199.

My introduction to 1199 coincided with the end of an era when Leon Davis, the founder, was the president. Davis, whose roots stemmed from the progressive Jewish community, began his career as a drugstore clerk. He saw the need for collective action in maintaining job security and adequate wages and, together with coworkers, established a union that represented all drugstore workers, including pharmacists. Unlike typical practices of its day, this union welcomed all workers, excluding no one because of skin color, religion, gender, or origin of birth.

As time went on, Davis saw a need to expand, and to that end, began to organize one of the most exploited groups of workers in America, unskilled hospital workers. Until the late 1950s, they were required to work up to sixty hours a week for less than minimum wage. Adding insult to injury, they were also forbidden to bargain collectively.

In organizing massive walkouts in 1959, 1962, and 1969, Davis was jailed twice—once for ten days and once for thirty days. However, his militancy significantly contributed to substantial increases in wages, job security, and benefits while adding tens of thousands to 1199 membership. Spurred by its success, thousands of professional and technical workers affiliated with 1199. Largely through these activities, the New York State law that denied healthcare workers the right to bargain collectively was repealed in 1963, followed by the repeal of a similar federal law in 1974.

Leon Davis retired in 1982. His handpicked successor, Doris Turner, took over the leadership until 1986, and in the process, almost destroyed the union. Turner began her career as a union leader during a historic fifty-six-day walkout in 1962, where she distinguished herself as a pugnacious, hardworking organizer. Following the strike's successful outcome, she went on to become a delegate, an organizer, and eventually an area director and vice president. As an African-American woman with distinguished rank-and-file credentials, she appeared to be a natural successor to Leon Davis, in a union where seventy-percent of its membership were African-American women.

Despite Turner's initial heroic efforts on behalf of 1199, as president she exhibited catastrophic character flaws. Following a long, hard struggle, she was removed from office by a united membership. "This Union used to be a black union with white leadership, now it's a black union with black leadership" was a Turner quote that resonated with many 1199 members. However, the emphasis on racial pride deteriorated into a concerted effort by Turner and her associates for power and wealth. Within two years after taking control, Turner had systematically removed most opposition in her quest for personal aggrandizement. Violence, intimidation, termination without cause, forced resignations, misuse of funds, ballot tampering, and suppression of free speech became the norm in a union that was founded on principles of trade-union democracy.

A wave of fear immobilized me during delegate assemblies where almost the entire body became an "amen corner" during Turner's rants. Opposition members had to gather in large groups to avoid personal intimidation, and a contingent had to remain in the parking lot to prevent tire slashing. One of the most regrettable moments in a lifetime of many mistakes was when, from the podium, Turner unleashed a tirade of antisemitism and called Bernie Minter a racist. I was too intimidated and afraid of openly challenging her. "I'm sorry,

Bernie." I realize now that there were enough good people among Turner supporters in that room to provide safety, had I done the right thing.

At that time, I did not have the maturity to respond honestly in an appropriate way to Turner. I met disagreements with personal attacks to express my displeasure. I would have described Turner as a terrible person in comparison to Bernie, a good person. This would not only have invited severe reactions among her supporters but would also have invalidated my argument. Here is what I would have liked to have said: "President Turner, as a loyal member of our great union, I am quite distressed by your remarks regarding Brother Minter. I have known Bernie Minter for many years and have learned much from his leadership, which entails a consistent and fearless effort in the struggle against racism and class injustice. I know that you will agree with me that unity is our greatest strength; however, your words about Brother Minter are at odds with this trade-union's principles, and I wish that, in the interest of our union, you would reconsider those words." Now, I can't imagine that my words would have moved Turner, and there is a good chance that I would have been removed from the meeting by her goon squad, but I would have given a clear message and not felt like a coward.

As part of her effort in opposition cleansing, Doris Turner fired Dennis Rivera, Eddie Kay, and Marshall Garcia from leadership positions in the early 1980s. Attempts to return 1199 to democratic principles entailed putting together a slate of progressives to elect Georgina Johnson. To run for office in 1199, one must be an 1199 member. Therefore Dennis, Eddie, and Marshall had to be affiliated with an 1199 bargaining unit. Dennis secured a job in a Manhattan institution only to have it revoked through Turner's influence. Enter Ira Marion. Ira was executive director of the AECOM Division of Substance Abuse Service and my boss. He hired these three guys, arguably among the leading innovators in the American trade union movement, as office clerks in his methadone program. They did a remarkable job—their supervisory evaluations were outstanding. Following our 1986 victory, all three men resumed well-deserved leadership positions in the union. In future discussions of trade union history, I hope that a glass will be raised to Ira Marion.

Our struggle to unseat Turner began in 1984 when we attempted to elect a good guy by the name of Joe Franklin. Although we failed, a fracture in Turner's "amen corner" began to emerge that ultimately blossomed into an outpouring of opposition to her tactics, leaving in its wake a small group of very vocal and, at times, hysterical Turner supporters. Eventually, they were recognized as incompatible with the will of the membership. In 1986, the largest voter turnout in the history of the union dismantled the Turner regime and elected Georgiana Johnson as president. Bernie proclaimed that this was the greatest trade union victory in the twentieth century, where criminals had taken over a union, and the members took it back.

The victory celebration and rally took place at the Beacon Theater attended by several hundred joyous 1199ers and about twenty-five diehard Turner supporters who were not very happy. Guests included New York's Governor Mario Cuomo, Manhattan Borough President Basil Patterson, and prominent activist, folk singer, and philosopher, Pete Seeger. After the Turner folks booed Cuomo and Seeger, Governor Cuomo addressed the dissenters. He asked them to express their displeasure as loud as they could. They did just that. When they finished, Cuomo asked the members who were happy with the election outcome to express their joy as loud as they could. The response was deafening, illuminating the collective will of the many in contrast to the rantings of the few.

The Doris Turner debacle did not materialize in the absence of paradoxical influences. There is enough criticism and blame to include others, including Leon Davis. Before Turner's ascendency to the presidency, the executive committee of 1199 included such luminaries as Moe Foner, Leon Davis, and Jesse Olson. Turner, as an area director and vice president, was a member of that committee but did not share in its decision-making. Operating in a "father knows best" manner, the elders wrote agendas and conducted union business without the interference of their "less sophisticated" colleagues—a manifestation of racism and a reminder that racism can be insidious. The motives of Davis, Foner, and Olson were in keeping with the standards of trade union principles. Still, their methods did not escape the evils of structural racism, racism that eventually produced fertile soil for the misguided and self-defeating method of fighting prejudice with prejudice. One does not fight racism with antisemitism. Turner and her associates did not understand this, but ultimately the rank-and-file membership of 1199 did.

Following the victory, life went on at AECOM. Leon Davis passed in 1990. Bernie delivered a beautiful eulogy at his memorial service and concluded it by singing the Kaddish in an excellent baritone voice. After knowing Bernie for many years, I discovered that he had been a cantor in the Jewish religion. A few months following Leon's passing, Bernie retired. He remained active in union affairs for a while but gradually succumbed to the inevitability of life, leaving a powerful message as a legacy to all who were privileged to have learned from him. His final request was a testament to the righteousness that guided his life. After thirty years of constant battle with the bosses at the Albert Einstein College of Medicine, he donated his remains to the medical school to enhance the learning of future medical practitioners. Bernie Minter was indeed a working-class hero.

The 1199 leadership of that period is now a memory. Joe James passed shortly after Bernie, followed by Marshall Garcia. Angela Doyle went on to serve as executive vice president, and Dennis Rivera went on to national prominence. Bernie and Joe's legacies are enshrined in two Bronx 1199 retiree chapters—The Bernie Minter chapter in the Northeast Bronx and the Joe James chapter in the South Bronx.

I felt my increased supervisory responsibilities compromised union integrity, so I resigned as a union delegate. I did, however, remain an active member of the bagaining unit, taking part in arbitrations and contract negotiations. Meanwhile, history reveals that Georgiana was perhaps in over her head and was replaced by Dennis Rivera, who moved on to higher aspirations and was replaced by our current president, George Gresham. None of these leaders were perfect. Like all human beings, they made mistakes, but they all served in the honored tradition of Leon Davis, who himself was not perfect.

Part Three
Redemption

11. NYU TAKES DOPEFIENDS

In 1984, my career took on a bit of transition during a home study prior to the arrival of Kevin. Flo Dines, a social worker from Children's Aid and Adoption Society, conducted the study. At one point, Flo asked Ilene what prompted her to contemplate a lifetime partnership with me. Without hesitation, Ilene responded, "Jim is a true friend, my best friend." Although not fully realizing the enormity of that statement at the time, I've come to experience it as a source of comfort, and I'm grateful. Despite the bumpy road on the way to a stable relationship, I knew that I had found someone who was honest, someone I could completely trust. Ilene created the life-sustaining space that enabled us to minister to each other, allowing me to love deeply without fear of abandonment. Thus, the preparation for Kevin's arrival was a happy and exciting time.

Following several interviews that completed the home study, Flo asked if I'd thought of taking advantage of 1199's benefit fund that would allow me to obtain a doctorate, tuition-free. My first reaction was that I didn't have the time, and besides, an MSW was considered the highest degree in social work. However, after discussing it with Ilene, Bill McGovern, and some colleagues, I concluded that this was a rare opportunity. Still, I had this gnawing feeling that I was getting into something that was over my head even though Ilene was quite supportive. Bill McGovern listened carefully as I verbalized my tightrope walk between fear and enthusiasm, then declared, "I am quite content in AA; Alcoholics Anonymous is my purpose in life. You are different. You can expand on what you've learned in AA to wondrous activities outside of AA. Get your doctorate." That was Gene Tice in a nutshell—good direction from someone I trusted.

I went on to apply to the doctoral program at NYU, and

after reading the acceptance letter, "We are pleased to inform you..." the fears and uncertainties returned. "These people take dopefiends in their doctoral program; how smart can they be?" Although pleased that I was accepted, I was frightened to death. What if they discovered that I'm really an imposter? Apparently, I still had some growing up to do.

Good fortune prevailed. Course work with a group of seasoned social workers, preparation for the comprehensive exam, and building a dissertation became a monumental learning experience. In the process, I had the privilege of associating with a group of mentors that included Lala Straussner, Deborah Padgett, and George Frank. Lala became a longtime friend, confidante, teacher, and adviser. Deborah, a committed progressive, had an amazing ability to address chaos and process it into clarity. I learned a lot from her. George, whose gentle wisdom provided reassurance in moments of doubt, left me with a firm conviction about whose side I was on.

The comprehensives are a seven-hour exam that encompasses material from two years of coursework—the godfather of the Ph.D. program. If you don't have a godfather, you don't get baptized, and if you don't pass the comprehensives, you don't get the degree. Unfortunately, I failed the comprehensives on my first attempt and had to wait a year to retake them, which was re-scheduled and held in a building on the downtown NYU campus. A few days before the test, after meeting with Lala, I decided to check out its location and discovered that the staff in that building were on strike and that there was a picket line outside. I panicked and ran to George Frank's office, where I blurted out, "George, I am a trade unionist and cannot cross a picket line." George was the department chair at that time. He calmly informed me that he was a trade unionist and wouldn't cross a picket line either. He said the exam must be taken on the scheduled date, and the powers-that-be wouldn't initiate a change in location, but if another location

could be provided, they would be amenable. After some negotiation, we were able to secure a spot from Reverend Garcia, an Episcopal priest who presided over a church in the
West Village.

The strike was settled the following day, rendering the location change unnecessary. I passed the comps, and upon com-
pletion of my dissertation, I graduated in 1997, yet another
milestone in my journey. An AA brother remarked, "That's
quite a trip, from dopefiend to doctor." It indeed was quite a
trip, and the outcome had everything to do with the people
that I encountered along the way, rather than any innate qualities I have. I showed up and was nurtured by gatherings of
good people, many of whom I named above.

The day after defending my dissertation and being awarded
the doctorate, I had the dubious responsibility of informing
Willie, a methadone client, that his pickup schedule was increased from five to six days a week due to his cocaine posi-
tives. Willie was not very pleased with this news because the
take-home methadone was an income-generating factor that
relaxed some of the constraints of poverty in his life. He loudly
exclaimed, "Motherfucker! You people don't do nothin' to help
people." I replied, "*Doctor* Motherfucker to you, tramp!" His
face brightened in a huge smile. "You got that PH thing? You
a doctor?" I answered, "Yes, I am." He wrapped his arms around
me in genuine delight, almost forgetting about the loss of his
take-home bottle.

Eventually, Willie detoxed from methadone and became associated with Narcotics Anonymous. His first two years in
the fellowship were a period of frequent relapse, but finally,
his recovery stabilized. He now attends meetings regularly,
drives a cab full time, and coaches youth basketball. Optimism reinforced!

Around this time, Bill McGovern's health began to deterio-
rate, necessitating frequent hospitalizations and a move from

cane to wheelchair. To accommodate his immobility, a Saturday morning "Big Book" meeting was started at his house in 2001. The "Big Book" is AA's principal text. This weekly meeting provided an in-depth study of AA principles amid an atmosphere of fellowship and camaraderie with much laughter. For me, it provided a basis for the ongoing study and interpretation of the Twelve Steps as a design for living and a guide to peace of mind and enlightenment.

Bill conducted weekly gatherings in his kitchen for six memorable years. Despite severe medical problems, his sharp perception and delightful sense of humor prevailed. Despite his agnostic tendencies, Bill was an observant Catholic. He kept a small holy water fount near the front door of his home. On my way out one morning, I noticed that the fount was dry. I asked Bill if he wanted me to stop by St. A's and get Father Dan to bless some water. He responded: "Fuck it, use tap water." That was Joe Flaherty revisited.

Bill presided at his last AA meeting in his hospital room with an assortment of AA brothers and sisters. We ended the meeting with the serenity prayer. Bill requested that we all leave because he was tired. The various systems in his body were beginning to shut down. He went into a coma the following day and passed two days later, November 9, 2007, leaving a legacy of love and service. Even though he kept tap water in his holy water fount and his language included curse words, his kitchen was a sacred place, and Bill McGovern was a holy man.

12. SOUTH BRONX OASIS

In 2007, the powers-that-be at AECOM decided that social workers were unnecessary in the treatment of addiction and dismantled the social work department in their Division of Substance Abuse service. At the age of seventy-one, after twenty-eight years of employment at AECOM, I was out of a job. I didn't realize it at the time, but AECOM did me a favor. I soon got a social work job at Fordham-Tremont, which was, at that time, considered the "Harvard" of mental health treatment in the Bronx. Unfortunately, I could no longer witness with an 1199 bargaining unit and had to assume a position of management. That was a very enlightening experience. It reinforced my belief that most union members take pride in their jobs, while most management representatives think that they occupy the moral high ground, and union workers must be monitored closely. I did not identify with management. This experience reinforced the answer to the question of which side I'm on. You can take the man out of the union, but you cannot take the union out of the man.

When I first received my doctorate, ten years before leaving AECOM, I was offered an administrative position with a pay raise and a significant reduction in benefits. I responded that I would gladly take the offer if I could remain in the bargaining unit. I was emphatically informed that I would have to leave the union, and if I did not take the offer, I would be making a grave professional error. Since I had a suspicion that the "promotion" could be a means of firing me, as I had been a thorn in management's side for several years, I elected to remain in 1199. In retrospect, I did the math and discovered that if I had left 1199 in 1997, I would have lost in the neighborhood of a quarter-million dollars in pension and medical benefits.

Shortly after leaving AECOM, in the hope of saying thanks for an enormously gratifying experience with 1199, I wrote a letter to the editor of "Our Life and Times," the 1199 SEIU Journal. In response, I received a phone call from an old friend, J.J. Johnson, who happened to be the Journal's chief editor. J.J. said that the letter was too long for the "Letters to the Editor," but he would like to run it as a feature article, reminiscent of Joe Flaherty's experience with the *Village Voice.* I was delighted. J.J. sent a team and a photographer to my new workplace. The article was published in the September 2007 issue. A couple of months later, J.J. called again to inform me that he submitted the article to the International Labor Communications Association and received word that it was awarded first-place in collective bargaining stories. Ilene and I went to Washington, D.C., where I received the 2007 Saul Miller Labor Journalism Award. The article was based on lessons learned from Bernie, Angie, Joe, and all the 1199 brothers and sisters with whom I was privileged to work.

Dr. Martha Sullivan, an old-school social worker and community organizer, was installed as executive director when I began employment at Fordham-Tremont. Sullivan's tenure embraced the tradition of social work's historic mission—service and activism. She introduced a Grand Rounds program that incorporated the cultural aspects of the community, paying homage to African-American and Latino history. Drawing on her years of experience in academia, she also provided the Fordham-Tremont staff an opportunity to keep abreast of ongoing developments in the treatment of mental illness and substance abuse in her Grand Rounds program.

I really admire Martha Sullivan. Her down-to-earth demeanor and remarkable intellect complement her deep concern for the poor and marginalized people whom she serves. She has the ability to listen carefully to all opinions and agree or disagree without raising her voice. As an African-American community activist, one of her deepest concerns is mass incarceration. She argues that jails and prisons have become a proxy for mental health treatment, particularly among young men of color, while reinforcing the proposition that alienation, a societal construct, is the major ingredient in mental health and addiction problems among inner-cities.

In 2013, celebrating Fordham-Tremont's thirty-fifth anniversary, Sullivan organized a borough-wide conference entitled "Men of Color and Mental Health: Moving from Alienation to Hope." I had the good fortune of working closely with her on this memorable endeavor.

Under Martha Sullivan's direction, I quickly became part of the Fordham-Tremont community and had the opportunity to share in the lives of many exceptional people, such as Ana. I first saw Ana in 2007, as she walked down the hallway, holding her mother's hand, her eyes downcast. She did not respond to my greeting, but her mom said hello while they moved on. I learned that Ana, 18 at the time, was a recent admission. Her initial psychosocial information revealed a history of foster care placements in early childhood, replete with physical and sexual abuse. The resulting severe anxiety disorder rendered her unable to speak publicly, and she was in constant fear.

Ana's mom was an active crack addict during Ana's early childhood. Eventually, through the guidance of Narcotics Anonymous, her mom got clean and sober and exhibited much spiritual growth but was consumed with guilt. After regaining custody, her primary goal in life was to help her daughter get rid of the darkness and despair that filled her soul. This quest led to several disappointing treatment experiences before a friend suggested that there were good people at Fordham-Tremont who would care for Ana.

Following an initial assessment, Ana was assigned to a social worker for ongoing psychotherapy and to a psychiatrist who prescribed and monitored antidepressant medication. Ana didn't feel safe, so her mom stayed with her during appointments. Lorie, her therapist, believed that under the circumstances, the mother's presence was not an obstacle to treatment. After two sessions with silent Ana and her mom, Lori assigned Ana to a group. Lori made it clear that her mom could go with her to the group and that Ana did not have to speak if she didn't want to.

Lorie's group welcomed them. For the first two months, Ana remained silent while listening attentively to the experiences and hopes of her fellow group members. At the beginning of the third month, Ana spoke, "My name is Ana." Her response was cathartic, a moment of joy. Ana then started to share and connect. Another milestone occurred after five months. Ana took the bus to Fordham-Tremont and began to attend group—by herself!

Eight years passed, and the last time I saw Ana was in 2015, just before I left Fordham-Tremont. Accompanied by her two-year-old child in a stroller, she told me that following a summer course requirement, she anticipated getting her BA from Leman College. Ana said she wanted to go on to graduate school and become a social worker, "like Lorie." In discussing her experience at Fordham-Tremont, Ana remarked that the group made her believe that she wasn't alone, that others understood her pain as much as she understood theirs, and they were able to help each other. She thanked me for being kind to her over the years and reported that her mom was also finishing college. A failed marriage had left Ana a single-parent mom, prompting her to declare, "I still don't do intimacy too well." This reminded me of Ariel Leve's proposition that "Refugees from childhood trauma are never (completely) at home in adulthood."

I met my "adopted" granddaughter, Celeste Benitez, during my tenure at AECOM. After a rather stormy early life, Celeste secured a bachelor's degree and began employment in community healthcare. She arrived at AECOM in 2003, as part of an HIV outreach team. Her energy level, her commitment to serve, and her remarkable intellect caught my attention.

I discovered that life was not always easy for Celeste: parental crack and alcohol addiction, juvenile detention, and gang affiliation were a significant part of her history. After years of addiction and criminal activity, her dad experienced a spiritual awakening during his last incarceration at Rikers Island. A Pentecostal activist visited him several times. The visitor's message focused on peace of mind and brotherhood. At first, Celeste's dad wasn't buying it. He responded to the message with a string of obscenities and spat at his visitor. The visitor returned and continued with his message. After thinking about his visitor, Mr. Benitez experienced a moment of clarity and began to entertain the possibility that there could be peace in his life. He ultimately realized that he wanted what his visitor had and subsequently got religion. He hasn't had a drink or a drug since.

When her dad was released from Rikers, Celeste was released from juvenile detention and planned to resume street life. Her dad had other plans. He employed former associates to ensure that Celeste attended school. That was a difficult time for Celeste because she didn't want to go to high school; the street was calling her. However, her natural curiosity about the world eventually took hold, and she went on to graduate high school, which paved the way for a professional career.

Celeste's dad, armed with his new conviction, interrupted a path that is all too common for young girls in poverty-stricken inner-city communities. Ann Weiss, a prominent author, educator, and social worker, depicts this phenomenon in a poem extrapolated from the original prose in one of her essays:

The young girls for whom childhood was a noisy blur of pain That had no name and from which there was no escape

Until...
At 12 or 13 There was The Street!
They were desired by boys and felt great.
They were given something to smoke or snort
And felt better - for a time.
Days and nights merged.
They went to school less and less and soon dropped out.
They became limp as leaves that the wind picks up
from here
And deposits there.
Sometimes they had a child or two "In care"
Or with a mother or an aunt to whom they had not
spoken in they can't remember how long.
They were in jail and out.
They were in rehab and out.
There were files with their names on them all over the city.
The young girls for whom childhood was a noisy blur of pain.

Despite a childhood that was *"a noisy blur of pain,"* Celeste escaped a common fate. After college and employment in healthcare, Celeste contemplated graduate school, but by this time, she was a single-parent mom and did not relish the added stress of graduate study. When discussing it with her immediate supervisor, she was told that if she remained on the job and did not pursue graduate work, they would promote her to Senior Coordinator. Although this was considered an in-house promotion and not reflective of a wage increase, it was a professional advancement. Drawing on lessons learned from my old PO, Gene Tice, I strongly advised Celeste to pursue graduate study, insisting that she was an absolute prime candidate for the social work profession. What followed was a conversation that further validated the need for paternal advice. Within our many conversations, I found out that Celeste had no living grandparents. I told her, "You need a grandpa to set you straight every once in a while, so I'll be your grandpa." She agreed, and we proceeded with an informal adoption. Celeste is now my "nieta."

Celeste completed social work school in 2008, while I was getting established at Fordham-Tremont, so she was hired as a social worker with little difficulty and assigned to my team. We worked closely for the next six years, which proved to be a wonderful experience for both of us. I had the immense pleasure of witnessing her spiritual development that encompassed knowledge of self with an abiding desire to serve. Celeste evolved into a serious Christian and community activist, firmly believing that she was called to do God's work in serving those with troubled lives. As she went along, Celeste retained her excellent street smarts and a fearless determination for justice, while gradually growing in the tradition of Jane Addams, Mary Richmond, and Bertha Reynolds—our social work foremothers.

Although Celeste is exceptional, Fordham-Tremont is home to many like-minded community residents who make up a significant proportion of program directors, medical staff, clinicians, clericals, security officers, and custodians. They have a stake in the community and provide a welcoming family environment that has great appeal to folks who seek their service. That established Fordham-Tremont as an exceptional learning opportunity for social work interns. Among graduate social work students from a variety of universities, Fordham-Tremont stood out as a "gem" for field placement. Despite current attempts to diminish service in a quest for bottom-line, profit-driven healthcare, social work schools continue to produce young, idealistic women and men whose primary goal is to serve.

My experience at Fordham-Tremont has added to my growing realization that service to others is strongly related to the joy of living. For many years I pursued what I thought were moral victories based on past resentments. An episode comes to mind: I was in a bullpen waiting to appear before a judge. There were ten other prisoners. I was out of cigarettes. The guy sitting on the floor next to me (the only other white guy there) opened a fresh pack and proceeded to light one up. I smiled, "Can I get one of them?" He responded dismissively, stating that he "only had nineteen left." I could not immediately challenge his rudeness, but for years I romanced a proper rebuttal, like forcing him to eat the remaining nineteen cigarettes. This resentment, among many others, had staying power that consumed much thought.

In looking back, the sustaining joyful moments in my life never involved moral victories but rather moments when I had the opportunity to do the right thing like returning the one-hundred-and-forty dollars to Sam, moments that have increased exponentially with sobriety. I realized that revenge and vengeance are tasty morsels that never achieve satisfaction and often result in spiritual indigestion.

Fordham-Tremont provided an opportunity to compare *getting even* to *giving* in my first attempt at poetry. One of my coworkers was not a very nice person, and I had an opportunity to put him in his place. And, I had an opportunity to provide a bowl of oatmeal to a hungry child and her mom. I experienced no satisfaction from the victory over the "not nice person" but had a completely different experience with the oatmeal. Any satisfaction gained from "getting even" quickly dissipates, while opportunities to serve are life-sustaining. Here is my poem titled *Shelf Life*:

The man is bellicose, arrogant,
Unknowledgeable,
Discourseably improper.
Needs to be taken down several pegs.
Tough work, must be done. Somebody should do it.

I rise to the task.
In elegant pursuit, make pointed reference to his:
Immaturity
Dullness of intellect
Incomplete character development
AND
Absence of ability to seek truth prior to mouth running.
Put him in his very own place.
Achieved moral superiority.
Witnessed his tongue-tied response.
I got that motherfucker!
Duration of satisfaction – fifteen seconds.
Little girl child holding a doll,
Eating potato chips.
Mom nearby, preoccupied with thoughts of:
Rich man landlord,
Perseverant in rent collection,
Indifferent to rats, roaches, falling ceiling.
Beats the homeless shelter – barely.
WHILE
Her Man pays homage to
The Law in its Majestic Equality
WHILE
Residing in 6x8 lodging
On an island called Rikers
Spent last dinero on a bag of weed and two Xanax
To take the edge off.
Promise unfulfilled.
Terms of existence reduce significance of a kid's breakfast.
Fifty cent bag of chips will have to do.
My, that's a pretty doll.
What's her name?
Girl child answers – Rosa.
Would you folks like some oatmeal?

Mom answers.
Oatmeal? That sounds good.
Instant oatmeal
Supplemented with brown sugar and coffee mate
Added to hot water. Nice breakfast for hungry people.
Mom says thank you.
Little ragamuffin with bright eyes, smiles
THANK YOU, MR. GRANDPA.
Duration of satisfaction – Lifetime.

Unfortunately, political realities invaded Fordham-Tremont; St. Barnabas was redefining itself and its affiliates as a health-care *business*. Within the St. Barnabas institution, Fordham-Tremont was considered a substantial revenue-producing entity, so to maximize this production of revenue, greater corporate control was needed, and changes occurred. Following the arrival of a new St Barnabas Psychiatry Department chair, Martha Sullivan left Fordham-Tremont. Under new leadership, the first order of business was to suspend Grand Rounds. That resulted in the cancelation of our annual celebration of Black History month and included the removal of Hispanic Heritage and Social Work month activities. The message was clear. Fordham-Tremont was in dire financial straits, and to avoid layoffs, we had to increase billable contacts and do away with non-income-generating activities. The social work intern program was canceled. The new chair of the psychiatry department micro-managed social work caseloads by implementing electronic medical records. Emails were sent: "This patient hasn't produced a billable contact in three months. Why wasn't the termination process started? This will require a corrective action."

Ironically, there was no concrete evidence that substantiated impending financial disaster at Fordham-Tremont. The growing movement to privatize and corporatize everything, from prisons to foreign policy, is not lost on the healthcare system. While not belaboring the well-documented weakness of United States healthcare, it is important to note that the United States spends much more on healthcare and has the least effective healthcare system of any other industrialized democracy in the world.

The move toward the corporatization of healthcare has negatively impacted service providers such as Fordham-Tremont. To keep up with the mandated number of billable visits, clinical staff routinely engages in much unpaid overtime, devoted to what many consider meaningless documentation that has little effect on the quality of treatment.

Joe is a remarkably talented clinician. His dedication and competence are reflected in numerous testimonies from clients and colleagues that span fifteen years of his employment at Fordham-Tremont. But Joe has dyslexia. Following increases in caseload size and increases in the amount of documentation, what began as a manageable problem grew to a quandary, which resulted in his having to spend four to five hours of unpaid overtime on an almost daily basis just to keep up with his paperwork. His colleagues also engaged in unpaid overtime, but not to the extent that Joe needed to.

St. Barnabas, reading the handwriting on the wall, recognized a potential lawsuit for unpaid overtime. They knew that the number of job requirements was impossible to complete in a normal workday, but they were unwilling to increase staff or pay overtime. Therefore, they demanded the use of timeclocks to reflect seven-hour workdays only. If Joe arrived at 8:00 am and stayed until 8:00 pm; he was instructed to wait until 9:00 am to punch in and 5:00 pm to punch out. If he chose to work off the clock, that was his decision. It created an administrative uneasiness that led to close scrutiny and much administrative pressure. The stress and hassle compelled Joe to resign from Fordham-Tremont, and he now works at another agency. A representative of the St. Barnabas administration stated that Joe was an incompetent clinician and is pleased that he is gone. As can be expected, his former clients and coworkers have a very different opinion.

One of Joe's former clients stopped by my office two months after Joe left. She related a story about a daughter who was going through a very defiant early adolescence. Mother/daughter sessions were started. During the initial session, the daughter released a tirade of verbal abuse directed at her mom. Joe's response was immediate. The mother recalled him saying, "You don't talk to your mother like that. Shame on you." According to the mother, that was the beginning of her daughter's growing up. She asked once, "When are we going to see Joe again? I need to talk to him." She is now in her senior year of high school, a lot less defiant and contemplating college. As her eyes welled up, the former client said, "I miss my 'Little Joe.'" Joe is 5'2".

What used to be considered "patients" or "clients" are now referred to as "consumers" or "customers." Indeed, "customer satisfaction" has replaced "patient satisfaction" in evaluation measurement. Frequent reminders that this was a "business," requiring precise documentation of services, and therefore swiping Medicaid cards became a primary activity. Therefore, treating the chart, not the person, was how we got paid. As this market-based system gained momentum, safety nets and opportunities gradually diminished. Remember the popular yoga program at the drug treatment center where I worked in 1969? That would never happen under today's rules because if you don't attach a treatment code and an appropriate diagnosis to an activity, you can't bill for the activity. That includes in-house AA meetings, client holiday parties, client choral groups, and all activities that do not directly produce revenue.

Despite the systemic deterioration of the welfare state,

Celeste and colleagues continue to provide valuable service to their communities, and our nation continues to produce more and more young people like them. I believe that the pendulum will swing back beyond the progressive changes of the 1960s. Eventually, the United States will have a publicly-owned and operated healthcare system and a criminal justice system that values redemption. I hope that I live to see it.

13. KALIEF

Kalief was a product of the South Bronx. He was admitted to Fordham-Tremont after a suicide attempt following a three-year imprisonment at Rikers Island for a crime that he did not commit. The circumstances of his life and death were grist for a *New Yorker* magazine article, a TV documentary, and Rikers Island reform efforts; he became a cause celeb of systemic inequities. But Kalief was much more than that.

His story does not begin with his imprisonment in 2010 but has roots in an alienated environment that frequently views police as predators rather than protectors. In addition to "brush your teeth, say please and thank you, and eat your vegetables," standard parental guidance for boys of color includes sharing methods for preventing injury or death when confronted by the police. Kalief and his friends adapted to this environment with the attitude that real respect for the law was optional.

Such was the case in 2009 when two of his friends stole a service van and crashed it into a parked car. Police arrived and "swept" the street of participants and bystanders. A sweep involves picking up everybody within proximity. The arrest of bystanders is not uncommon in the South Bronx. Kalief was a bystander. He was charged with car theft and ultimately given the choice of either facing felony charges that could lead to years of incarceration or admit guilt as a youthful offender and get probation. Like countless young people of color in similar situations, he chose the latter, unaware of the potential repercussions of this decision.

A year later, at the age of sixteen, Kalief was arrested for stealing a backpack. The well-documented circumstances of this alleged crime reveal a series of inconsistencies that question the validity of the arrest. However, police considered Kalief a likely suspect, as he had a "prior." He was charged and sent to Rikers Island, where he remained for the next three years in pre-trial detention.

Kalief's situation is not unusual in the Bronx, New York City's poorest borough where defendants have routinely spent years awaiting trial. The Bronx Defenders, an underpaid, overworked group of legal professionals, are attempting to rectify this problem. Scott Levy, an attorney associated with this group, declares, "Waits for a trial are so long that it effectively makes the right to a trial meaningless." The Bronx Defenders' work is an uphill battle. Several current and former members of the New York City Police Department contend that the police department pressures officers to meet arrest quotas in neighborhoods of color, resulting in arrests for trivial matters and, in some cases, for crimes that the arrestees did not commit. The upper echelon of the NYPD vehemently denies this practice and has promised to sanction supervisors who enforce quotas, yet evidence of this practice continues. Indeed, there are currently more than 250,000 arrests per year in the Bronx, while court staff can dispose of a little over 600.

Consequently, prosecutors, who have the burden of processing hundreds of thousands of cases, regularly attempt to pressure defendants to plead guilty to a lesser crime. As in Kalief's case, not all defendants are guilty of committing a crime, but the inability to make bail becomes a sound reason to take a plea. His bail was set at $3,000. His mother didn't have the money. His father refused to put up the bail. When Jay-Z asked him why he didn't bail his son out, the father replied, "I didn't want to."

Upon arrival at Rikers, gang members aggressively confronted Kalief in an attempt to recruit him. From my own prison days, I know what this is like and young Kalief was not prepared for it. Prior to his arrest and incarceration problems with authority were limited to adolescent mischief such as cutting classes and occasional weed smoking, a far cry from gangs and hard drugs. His limited experience on the streets of the South Bronx didn't prepare him with the skills needed to negotiate life on Rikers Island. He learned that gangs and incompetent correction officers are a powerful force at Rikers. Following his refusal to join a gang, a gang leader spat in his face and Kalief retaliated by punching his assailant in the face, which was immediately followed by an attack involving several gang members. Correction officers' attempted to restore order by placing Kalief in solitary confinement, his first trip to the "bing," which ultimately totaled twenty-three months of his three-year imprisonment.

I first met Kalief in November 2013, when he was admitted to Fordham-Tremont, the clinic where I worked. He referred to photos of my two African-American sons, and asked "Is your wife a black woman?"

I answered, "No, we adopted the boys when they were babies."

He smiled and said, "That's cool."

And then he visibly relaxed and told me a story that revealed the true nature of the criminal justice system in the Bronx. A proper investigation would have corroborated Kalief's innocence, but an intolerable, overburdened system did not have the means to provide justice for this African-American boy. I don't believe that I ever encountered a person who showed such strength of character under such horrendous circumstances. He could have pleaded guilty to a lesser crime and gotten immediate release, but because he insisted on his innocence, he remained in jail. Character strength relegated Kalief to the status of "fish out of water" at Rikers. His refusal to join a gang resulted in beatings by gang members. He was isolated and subjected to starvation. He was beaten by correction officers followed by several suicide attempts. Before his imprisonment, Kalief had no history of psychiatric disturbance; prior to his release and after his release he exhibited characteristics of severe post traumatic stress disorder.

After the isolation and complete lack of intellectual stimulation at Rikers, he seemed to be finding his feet and thriving in college while his innate intellectual curiosity gradually reawakened. He would often stop by my office where I had in hand standard ingredients conducive to conversation —coffee pot and tea kettle. He would have a cup of tea and I would have a cup of coffee. I was amazed and delighted as I witnessed Kalief discover reading treasures such as Michele Alexander's *The New Jim Crow*, W.E.B. Du Bois *The Souls of Black Folk*, and Martin Luther King, Jr.'s sermons in *A Knock at Midnight*, which he devoured at home and further explored in conversation.

Because of his father's religious extremism and bigotry, Kalief viewed religion with skepticism and suspicion. King's social gospel however, provided a broader look at religion and a greater understanding of King's impact on American history. He also expressed genuine admiration for Du Bois and Alexander, remarking that Du Bois' prophetic words, "The problem of the twentieth century is the problem of the color line," was a theme recaptured by Alexander that had relevance in the 21st century. Kalief's interest in African-American history was also apparent in his appreciation of original rhythm and blues artists. He spoke reverently of Ruth Brown, Joe Turner, and Big Momma Thornton, his favorites. I took great pride in hearing that he was on the Dean's List at Bronx Community College.

Following a featured article in The New Yorker and an appearance on "The View," Kalief began unwittingly to assume the status of media celebrity. Some of the media involvement was positive, such as in exposing the inhumane conditions at Rikers, which led to the end of solitary confinement for teenagers. As a result of media publications, an anonymous donor paid for Kalief's college tuition.

But Kalief was still fragile and his situation was precarious. He was homeless, because of an ongoing conflict that he had with his father. His parents were divorced, and although his father didn't reside there, he held title to the family home, paid the mortgage, and therefore determined who could live there. Kalief's mom reluctantly went along with this decision, thinking that she didn't have a choice. Her former husband stated that if he caught Kalief in the house, the whole family would get kicked out. Nevertheless, Kalief's mom allowed him to stay in the home for short periods while managing to keep his father unaware. In attempting to survive this precarious situation, Kalief, at times, "couch-surfed" with friends and with a cousin; other times, he stayed on the streets. The paradox of his situation was that, on the one hand, he was on the Dean's List and getting important media attention, but on the other hand, he was homeless and trying to recover from the trauma of his unjust imprisonment.

I arrived at work the morning following the news of Kalief's suicide and joined the team of social workers who knew and loved him. Tom Wolfe, Kalief's therapist, in addition to being a social worker, is an ordained Methodist minister. Amid tears, Tom led us in prayer. It seemed that the entire staff was in shock, a staff that was not unfamiliar with violence and death among clients.

At that moment, in the depth of my own grief, I didn't think that I would be blamed and then fired—but that is what happened. Nevertheless, I was acutely aware of the fact that Kalief entered my life following an ordeal that conceivably would have destroyed most people. He was wounded, but he was not without determination and not without an eloquent capacity for moral judgment. His life ended because of societal forces over which he had no control. The system killed him, not just the criminal justice system, but the entire structure of his world where he was programmed to be the "other," with significant limitations in opportunities and rights.

Throughout my years as a social worker, I have seen much tragedy. Client suicides, violent deaths, and the AIDS crisis have all contributed to personal feelings of grief and despair. And still, Kalief's death stands out. He provided a direct illumination of humanity at its highest level. He was destined for greatness. His passing left me with an emptiness that one can only imagine from the loss of a child.

This could be where my story ends. I was an unemployed 78-year-old social worker, depressed, angry, and grief-stricken. But just like Kalief's story didn't begin with a backpack arrest, mine doesn't end with leaving Fordham-Tremont. I thought back to my childhood and questioned, "What would the Irish nun do?"

I answered, "She would go on with her life in service to others."

I have work to do.

ACKNOWLEDGEMENTS

The god of my misunderstanding has been good to me.

Writing a book is hard. Without the direction, strength, and wisdom provided by many remarkable people the final product never would have materialized. First and foremost my wife Ilene—soulmate, partner, and best friend whose encouragement and constructive guidance has been an anchor. Her commitment to my wellbeing and the reliability of her down-to-earth honesty provided energy and enthusiasm for my work in writing this book. Thank you, Ilene.

My sons and daughter-in-law: Kevin, Brian, and Diana have been incredibly consistent in support and interest. Tragically, we lost our beloved Brian who passed on February 26, 2020. Kevin and Diana, in what can be described as a parents/children role reversal, took charge in this heartbreaking, painful event. Thank you, Kevin and Diana. And thank you Brian, not only for your feedback on the manuscript but for being the amazing son that you were. You will always be in my heart.

Special thanks to Dr. Mindy Fullilove, a treasured friend who provided mentorship and guidance based on her many years as a scholar, author, educator, psychiatrist, and community activist. However, Mindy's best contribution to this book was her insistence that I join a writing group that she helped develop twenty years ago. Thank you, Mindy.

In looking back over the last five years that I've been a member of this group the words of the great philosopher and basketball coach, John Wooden, come to mind: *"When you stop learning, you stop living."* Starting at age seventy-eight this group became my teachers. At the beginning of my involvement with the group, I was dealing with issues following the suicide of a very special person, and the forced retirement from a job and profession that I loved. Furthermore, I believed that I was in over my head with this group. But as I began to witness and ultimately contribute to the creative process of these remarkable people while sharing my own work, magic happened. The doldrums and self-doubt faded. I was becoming a writer while Maggie Thompson's prophecy was becoming a reality. Maggie, Mindy's mom, wrote a beautifully inspiring memoir at the age of ninety-one; in the process she advised old folks to write, "It makes you feel better," claiming that writing rescued her—just as the group rescued me. Thank you, Simon Fortin, Ann Burack-Weiss, Maura Spiegel, Craig Irvine, Kelli Harding, John Kavanaugh, Jack Saul, Helena Hansen, and Didi Heller.

It is difficult to find words to adequately describe the editing skills of Susan Hasho. She has an amazing ability to extract harmony from disorder in a manner that utilizes the skills of the writer. Moreover, Susan has innate qualities that add dimension to her work—kindness, sense of humor, and capacity for listening to and respecting others. Thank you, Susan.

I would be remiss if I didn't recognize my AA sisters and brothers as a contributing factor in completing the book. Within the current troubled world, amplified and aggravated by personal tragedy, I have frequent opportunities to witness with a towering and prodigious group of people whose collective spirit of hope, optimism, and love abounds. Thank you, Walt, John, Linda, Jack, Evelyn, Ron, Sean, Doug, Peter, Rita, Eddie, Elenore, Helen, Alan, Kevin, Susan, and others whose names escape immediate recall but whose incorporeal presence remains.

CPSIA information can be obtained
at www.ICGtesting.com
Printed in the USA
LVHW040004030221
678222LV00005B/724